THE BULLDOG

Diane Morgan

The Bulldog
An Interpet Book

Project Team
Editor: Stephanie Fornino
Copy Editor: Jessica White
Indexer: Dianne Schneider
Design: Stephanie Krautheim
Series Design: Mada Design
Series Originator: Dominique De Vito

First published in United Kingdom 2008 by
Interpet Publishing
Vincent Lane
Dorking
Surrey
RH4 3YX

United Kingdom Editorial Team
Hannah Turner
Nicola Parker

ISBN   978 1 84286 170 7

Printed and bound in China

This book has been published with the intent to provide accurate and authoritative information in regard to the subject matter within. While every reasonable precaution has been taken in preparation of this book, the author and publisher expressly disclaim responsibility for any errors, omissions, or adverse effects arising from the use or application of the information contained herein. The techniques and suggestions are used at the reader's discretion and are not to be considered a substitute for veterinary care. If you suspect a medical problem, consult your veterinarian.

INTERPET
PUBLISHING

www.interpet.co.uk

TABLE OF CONTENTS

HISTORY
of the Bulldog

The Bulldog is one of the world's most universally recognised and beloved breeds. He has long been one of the symbols of Britain, partly because famous "John Bull," the English counterpart of Uncle Sam, looked rather like a Bulldog in a vest, and partly because he is supposed to resemble the English in terms of his determination and courage.

The first description of the Bulldog appeared in 1500, when a certain W. Wulcher referred to the breed as the "Bondogge" in reference to the practice of Bulldogs being tied up (bonded) with other dogs. Shakespeare also mentioned the breed in his play *King Henry VI*, although the actual term "Bulldog" first appeared in writing in 1609. However, it was only in the 1630s that the breed started to look like the present-day Bulldog. Some people call the Bulldog the "English" Bulldog, perhaps as opposed to the French Bulldog or the American Bulldog, but the official name of this breed is simply "Bulldog." Those who admire and own Bulldogs are called Bulldoggers.

REALLY ANCIENT BULLDOG HISTORY

As hard as it may be to believe, once there was a world without Bulldogs, although it wasn't a world any of us would want to live in. (Before there were Bulldogs, there was no central heating. I'm not saying there's a cause and effect relationship here, but it is a fact.)

At any rate, to better know who the Bulldog is, we should take a look at his relatives. Wolves, jackals, foxes, and dogs are all members of the family Canidae, and wolves and dogs are so close as to share the same species name, *Canis lupus*. This means that they can interbreed and have fertile offspring, although left to their own devices, wolves and dogs keep to their own separate communities. They have a different culture and a wildly different outlook on life. Their main difference is philosophic: Dogs like people and wolves don't. Current dogs are descended from certain wolves who had nothing better to do

Bulldogs are mastiff-type dogs who were most likely descended from the Tibetan Mastiff.

than hang around stone-age camp fires hoping for a handout. They must have received them, because modern dogs are still begging for food with roughly equal success.

Bulldogs are mastiff-type dogs, and like all such animals, they are probably descended from the large and dangerous Tibetan Mastiff. How Tibetan Mastiffs arrived in Britain is a mystery. Some speculate that the Phoenicians brought them there, although this is debatable, because the Phoenicians were sailors and Tibet is landlocked. It is probably more accurate to say that the Bulldog's ancestors were the great Molossian Mastiffs. These European war dogs probably owe their heritage to the Tibetan Mastiff somewhere along the line, but the actual line of descent is shrouded in mystery.

The "Sport" of Bullbaiting

It's one of the ironies of history that this noble, gentle breed has a dark past, much of which is tied up in the cruel "sport" of bullbaiting. This activity has its roots in ancient Crete, Greece, and Rome. In those cultures, the bull was actually considered sacred, and a great number of "games" and sacrifices were devised around him. In the beginning, people were used. Later, at least in some locations, dogs took their place. Sometime in the thirteenth century, the Earl Warren, an English lord, happened to notice a group of dogs chasing a bull down the street. He thought it was so amusing that he arranged for the spectacle to be repeated every year six weeks before Christmas.

Between the 13th and 19th centuries, the horrible sports of bull and bearbaiting were spectacles that people of all ages and classes enjoyed. In fact, it was England's most popular sport, and it received government support under King John, one of England's worst kings. (He was so bad that the British never attempted another King John.)

Cattle and dogs have always shared history. Some dog breeds were developed to herd cattle, others to guard them. Bulldogs were bred, at least after a time, to fight them. The first Bulldogs, however, may have been real working dogs whose job was to restrain livestock about to be slaughtered. Eventually, this ugly but perhaps necessary work devolved into a "sport" in which a dog would sneak up on a tethered bull and attempt to grab him by the nose in order to drag him to the ground. The bull, naturally, would defend himself vigorously with his horns. Very often, both combatants would end up dead or seriously injured, which one must suppose was part of the fun. Rules for the "sport" varied from place to place. In one locality, the bull was untethered, and the dog had to pull the bull backward around the ring. In another

National Kennel Clubs

Australia
www.ankc.aust.com

Canada
www.ckc.ca

Denmark
www.dansk-kennel-klub.dk/

Finland
www.kennelliitto.fi/

Japan
www.jkc.or.jp/index_e.html

New Zealand
www.nzkc.org.nz

Norway
www.nkk.no/

Portugal
www.cpc.pt/

Sweden
www.skk.se/

United Kingdom
www.the-kennel-club.org.uk

United States
www.akc.org

The first Bulldogs may have been real working dogs whose main job was to restrain livestock.

The KC

The Kennel Club's members are individual persons. The membership of the Kennel Club is restricted to a maximum of 1,500 UK members in addition to 50 overseas members and a small number of honorary life members. The Kennel Club promotes responsible dog ownership and works on important issues like canine health and welfare.

The American Kennel Club (AKC), founded in 1884, is the most influential dog club in the United States. The AKC is a "club of clubs," meaning that its members are other kennel clubs, not individual people. The AKC registers purebred dogs, supervises dog shows, and is concerned with all dog-related matters, including public education and legislation. It collects and publishes the official standards for all of its recognised breeds.

place, the dog was supposed to pin the bull and throw him to the ground while the bull would attempt to disembowel the dog. The handlers tried to catch the thrown dogs, with varying degrees of success. The winning dog was the one who held on the longest. Those who had no saner use for their disposable income bet enormous amounts of money on this "game."

As time went on, it was clear which type of dogs had the best luck against bulls. Mastiffs were used at first, but their large size and off-the-ground stance made them an easy target for the desperate, benighted bulls. The gentlemanly dog whom we know as the Bulldog today was bred down from the Mastiff specifically and solely to participate in this dreadful activity.

The first essential quality was a low-to-the-ground animal, to minimise the chances of the bull's horn being inserted between the dog's belly and the ground. A dog with powerful shoulders and great strength of jaw was obviously required, as well as one with fierce tenacity and the ability to fight on through pain. And if the dog was tossed in the air, it helped to have a short, strong back and less-developed hindquarters to minimise the damage. Good padding around the ribcage helped prevent serious injuries when the animal hit the earth.

Early breeders used all kinds of terrible methods to create the kind of dog they wanted. They encouraged what most people consider deformities and even made puppies wear stiff masks to distort their features even more. They crammed them into kennels with insufficient headroom to force them even lower to the ground. Of course, such body alterations aren't genetically transferable, but early breeders didn't know what kinds of things were inherited and what weren't. They also used torture and cruelty to create a vicious, pain-resistant fighting animal.

The Bulldog's jaw is such an unusual-looking piece of anatomy that it cries out for explanation. The lower jaw, or mandible, extends beyond the front jaw. In most breeds, this is a fault because it truly does interfere with proper chewing. However, it has historic importance. An undershot jaw enabled the Bulldog to grab the bull at any point, clamp down, and hang on. Once the Bulldog got a grip, the jaws "locked." This is not the gentle mouth of a retriever! While hanging on, the animal was still able to breathe, because the nose was set back from the jaw. The Bulldog could actually hang on until the bull bled to death.

That Funny Face

The appeal of Bulldogs does not lie in the fact that they were good at battling bulls. No, it's their face that we love most, and researchers at the University of Western Australia may have discovered the reason. They performed a study to examine the relationship between skull size in dogs and the position, dimensions, and structure of the eyes and nose. They found that dogs with long noses have pronounced "visual streaks," a concentration of cells that provides more sensitivity of movement along a horizontal field. Short-nosed animals (like people) have cells congregating around a central area instead that allow better up-close focus. Bulldogs are more similar to people than to most other dogs in this regard. These short-faced dogs are less likely to be efficient hunters, but they are more likely to watch things closely — things like the faces of their owners. Their commitment is to their human family, not their ancestral pack. This may be one reason why long-nosed sight hounds tend to be more aloof and less attentive to their owner's facial expressions than the Bulldog and similar short-nosed breeds.

Even the wrinkles had a purpose, at least according to some authors. The many folds of the skin permitted the shed blood of the bull to run around the dog's face rather than directly into his eyes. There's also an equally shaky theory that the loose jowls of the Bulldog smothered the bull while the dog was hanging on. It's truer to say that the Bulldog seized the bull by the nostrils and shut off the air supply that way. If you are wondering how your own Bulldog could have managed any of this, it's important to remember that the first Bulldogs were a less exaggerated version of today's models, who usually have to be born by a caesarean section. (The head is the portion of the anatomy to which the most attention is paid in the show ring.)

Bullbaiting was finally made illegal in England in 1835, but it continued underground for many years, just as dog fighting does in the modern world.

THE BULLDOG IN ENGLAND

While the abolition of bullbaiting was a great relief to the bulls and Bulldogs, the breed itself, without an official "use," slowly began to decline. But then something magical happened: the invention of the dog show in the second half of the 19th century. Dog shows were all the excuse aficionados of the breed needed to begin breeding their beloved breed again. However, there was a problem. The first Bulldogs were noble, courageous, and powerful, but they were also incredibly vicious. As a result, breeders were in a quandary. They loved the positive qualities of the breed, but who

Bulldogs at Crufts

Great interest in the Bulldog was caused when "King Dick" owned by Jacob Lamphier was exhibited at the Birmingham Show in 1861. He is now regarded as the forerunner of the type seen today.
By the time the Crufts dog show came into being in 1891 Bulldogs had already been exhibited for thirty years. The only Bulldog ever to win Best In Show at Crufts was CH. Noways Chuckles owned and bred by John and Marjorie Barnard in 1952.

wanted a dog who couldn't be taken out in public?

It dawned on these breeders that whatever use Bulldogs had served in the past was irrelevant. Viciousness had been bred into Bulldogs, and it could be bred out. The premier person responsible for this was Bill George, a breeder who named his kennel the Canine Castle. Other famous early breeders were F.G.W. Crayer, J.S. Pybus Sellon, F.W. Crowther, W.H. Sprague, and A.E. Vicary.

The first written Bulldog standard was drafted in 1864. The Bulldog Club was founded in 1874 and incorporated one year later as the Bulldog Club Inc. This makes the Bulldog Club the oldest breed club in the world. A Standard of Perfection was formulated and published in England in 1875. The club also produces an illustrated magazine twice a year called, simply, *The Bulldog*. The first show for the breed was held in Birmingham, England in 1860. The best of the early Bulldog show animals was a dog with the name of Old King Dick. This dog's genes are present even today in some lines.

The Bulldog Club's stated goals include:
- To promote the breeding of pure Bulldogs of the true type and to urge the adoption of such type upon breeders, judges, committees, and promoters of canine exhibitions.
- To publish and promulgate the true type of pure Bulldogs by means of a standard description of its correct appearance and the various characteristic points in detail of a perfectly formed Bulldog, for uniform adoption as the sole standard of excellence, and for the guidance of breeders and of judges in awarding prizes and distinctions of merit and dog shows or other canine competitions.
- To promote information on canine subjects by means of lectures, discussions, the editing of a journal, books, periodicals, correspondence, drawings, or otherwise.
- To promote, hold, or arrange either independently or in connection with other persons, exhibitions, dog shows and matches, with the object of encouraging the breeding and propagation of the true English Bulldog.

Another UK club, in some ways established as a rival to the Bulldog Club, is the British Bulldog Club, founded in 1892. Its stated aims are:
- To encourage and promote the breeding of Bulldogs.
- To give prizes, support, and hold exhibitions of Bulldogs.

THE BULLDOG IN THE UNITED STATES

Bulldogs appear to have been present in America as early as 1774. They were accepted into the American Kennel Club in 1886. The first registered Bulldog was simply named Bob. The Bulldog Club of America was then established in 1890 and incorporated under the laws of the state of New York on February 29, 1904. The framers of its constitution stated its purposes to be as follows:

- To maintain a standard of excellence for the guidance of breeders, owners, and judges.
- To improve the breed through encouragement of effort directed toward approach to, or attainment of, the degree of excellence set forth in the standard of the Bulldog breed.
- To stimulate interest in competitive public showings of Bulldogs.
- To further the interests of the Breed.
- To work for the general good of breeders, owners, and exhibitors of Bulldogs.

Early breeders in the United States include John H. Matthews of New York City, R.B. Sawyer of Milwaukee, E. Sheffield Porter of New Haven, and C.G. Cugle of Hartford. The first Bulldog "show dog" in this country was a fellow named Donald. The first Bulldog to become an American Kennel Club champion was a dog by the name of Robinson Crusoe. He achieved the title in 1888.

One of the most famous Bulldogs in the United States is the brindle and white Sergeant Chesty XI, the official mascot of Marine Barracks Washington D.C. Her "call name" is Molly, which comes from the term "Molly Marines," the name given to the first women in the United States Marine Corps.

The abolition of bullbaiting in 1835 led to the development of the Bulldog as a show dog.

straight line at right angles with the stop, which is the place where the muzzle meets the main part of the skull. The eyelids should cover the whites of the eye, and no haw should be visible. (The haw is the red part of the eye you might see in a Bloodhound.)

The Kennel Club standard adds that any dogs showing signs of respiratory distress are highly undesirable.

The ears should be thin and small. They should be set high—as far from the eyes as possible. The front inner edge of each ear should join the outline of the skull at the top back corner of the skull. While various ear shapes occur, the most desirable is the "rose ear." The rose folds inward at the back lower edge, while the upper edges curve outward and backward, actually showing part of the inside. In any case, upright, prick ears, or button ears are not desirable.

The skull should be very big, broad, and square. If you measure the circumference of the skull in front of the ears, it should at least equal the height of the dog at the shoulders. If you look at the head from the front, it should appear very high and very short from the point of the nose to the occiput, the point at the back of the skull. The forehead should be flat and not too prominent; it shouldn't overhang the face.

The cheeks should be well rounded and protrude outward beyond the eyes. The stop should be broad, deep, and very well defined, and there should be a groove between the eyes. There should be an indentation extending up the middle of the forehead, dividing the head vertically right up to the top of the skull. The face should be extremely short, with a short, broad, very upturned muzzle. The nose should be large, broad, and black. Its tip should be as short as possible and set back deeply between the eyes. The distance from the bottom of the stop to the tip of the nose should not be longer than the distance from the tip of the nose to the edge of the underlip. The nostrils should be wide, large, and black, with a well-defined line between them. The lips should be thick, broad, hanging, and deep. In fact, they should overhang the lower jaw at each side. They join the underlip in the front and should cover (or almost cover) the teeth. (In the ideal Bulldog, you shouldn't notice the teeth when his mouth is closed.) The jaw should be massive, broad, square, and undershot. That means it should project out a considerable distance from the upper jaw. It should also turn up. The teeth should be big and strong, with the canine teeth set wide

Chest

While a Bulldog reaches his full height by about four months, his head and chest don't start to catch up until he's about eight to nine months old. These continue to develop until the Bulldog is three or four years of age.

The wrinkle over the nose is called the "nose rope."

The stifle (the joint between the thigh and "second thigh") should turn out slightly, which causes the hocks to approach each other and the hind feet to turn outward. As with the front feet, the hind feet should be medium in size but compact. The compact toes should have high knuckles and short, stubby nails.

Coat and Skin

The coat should be straight, short, smooth, and flat, with a fine texture and glossy appearance. The skin should be soft and loose, especially around the shoulders. There should be plenty of heavy wrinkles around the head and face. From jaw to chest should hang two loose folds called dewlaps.

Coat Colour

According to the Kennel Club, permitted colours (no order given) include whole ("solid") or smut. ("Smut" means a solid colour with a black mask or muzzle.) The only whole colours allowed are brindles; reds with their various shades; fawns, fallows, etc.; white; and pied (i.e., a combination of white with any of the foregoing colours). Dudley (brown), black, or black with tan are highly undesirable. The acceptable colours should be pure and brilliant.

Bulldogs fanciers who follow the American Kennel Club standard like pure, brilliant coat colours, and the following colours are listed in order of preference: (1) red brindle; (2) other brindles; (3) solid white; (4) solid red, fawn, or fallow; (5) piebald (large patches of two or more colours). However, a good clear piebald is considered better than a "muddy" brindle. Solid black is not desirable, although it can appear in piebald patches. The best brindles have a fine, even, equal distribution of the composite colours. A small patch of white is allowed on brindles and solid-

The Bulldog has a kind, peaceful, and courageous temperament.

coloured dogs. In piebalds, the colour patches should be well defined, symmetrically distributed, and of pure colour.

Gait

The Bulldog moves in a peculiar loose-jointed, shuffling way. It's a kind of sidewise motion that gives a characteristic "roll." Despite this unusual gait, the Bulldog must move in a free, unrestrained, vigorous manner.

The Kennel Club standard reads a bit differently, describing the moving Bulldog's gait as peculiarly heavy and constrained. He should appear to walk with short, quick steps on the tips of his toes, hind feet not lifted high, appearing to skim the ground, and running with one or the other shoulder rather advanced. At the same time, the British standard emphasises that soundness of movement is of the extremely important.

Temperament

The Bulldog is kind, peaceful, and courageous. All of these attributes should reveal themselves in his expression and behaviour.

CHARACTER AND TEMPERAMENT

Appearance isn't the only factor contributing to the Bulldog's

Supervision and guidelines provide the keys to a successful relationship between children and Bulldogs.

infinite charm. I would like to refer to his personality, but that word is much too weak. The Bulldog has more than personality; he has character—a unique character. He is solid, sensible, and patient. The Bulldog is not a push-button kind of guy who will cater to your every whim, but he'll make a good-faith effort to figure you out—at least to the point where you're waiting on him, rather than vice versa.

The Bulldog is not for everyone. Control freaks who need a push-button dog would do better with a different breed. This is a stubborn dog who ranks low on every "trainability scale" ever devised, although females are probably a little more trainable than males (especially in terms of housetraining) and may respond better to the subtle cues of obedience work. If your previous dog was a retriever or a German Shepherd, you're in for a big shock, but not necessarily an unpleasant one. If you like to take things easy and enjoy the simpler pleasures of life, the Bulldog is for you. Senior citizens, people with physical disabilities, and those who don't feel the need to plunge into the wilderness every weekend connect especially well with the sedate, ultra-civilised Bulldog.

The Bulldog is one of the safest and most reliable dogs around

children because of his pretty limitless tolerance and fondness for small ones. This doesn't mean a child should ever be allowed to tease or abuse a Bulldog, of course. Fortunately, Bulldog breeders have done a thorough job of breeding out aggression in a breed whose powerful jaws make an aggressive Bulldog a very dangerous one.

As gentle as they are, however, a Bulldog will not back down from a fight if one is forced upon him, and if necessary he will defend his family to the utmost. This dog does not know fear. In some cases, Bulldogs don't like other dogs, especially when males are involved. If you have other pets, you'll need to socialise your Bulldog carefully.

There are no major differences in the temperament of males and females; individual differences count for much more than gender stereotypes. Different owners will have different experiences with their Bulldogs, regardless of gender.

Your Child and Your Dog

While dogs and kids are born to be friends, common sense tells us that supervision and guidelines are the keys to happiness. Puppies are especially at risk from overexuberant or cruel children. Always remember that you are the parent and you are the dog's owner, so the ultimate responsibility for your Bulldog's welfare is yours. The Bulldog is on your side, however! Bulldogs love children and only need to be given an opportunity to make friends. Some animal experts say that the best time to add a dog to your family is when the children are between seven and nine years old, as toddlers can injure or be injured easily by a puppy. In my opinion, if you are watchful, there's no reason whatsoever why a younger child cannot enjoy the family Bulldog. Besides, recent studies have shown that early childhood exposure to pets reduces the chances of children developing all kinds of allergies, not just allergies to pets!

Along with the joys of puppy ownership, kids can learn responsibility. Picking up dog toys, walking the pup, straightening the bed, riding along to the vet surgery, and helping to prepare the puppy's meals are all ways to teach responsibility and help cement the bond between child and dog. Older children can also participate in training. All children should also be aware of the "five no's" of puppy ownership: no hitting or screaming, no dragging, no table feeding, no pestering, and no hugging (which sometimes turns into unintentional strangling — at least that's how the dog sees it).

Always remember that the adult member of the family is responsible for the Bulldog's well-being. While having a pet is a good way for children to learn responsibility, the pet should not pay the price if the child forgets or becomes bored with the dog. Adults, not children, are ultimately responsible for making sure the dog is fed, walked, vetted, and loved.

The following are some guidelines to help your child and your Bulldog live in harmony.

• Obviously, striking a puppy is cruel and counterproductive. Causing pain to another being is not a good way to induce either love or obedience, only resentment and fear. Bulldogs are bred to have excellent dispositions and are tolerant to pain, but they have tender feelings that can be permanently damaged by violence to their persons. Unfortunately, a Bulldog is so unusual-looking that some children may be frightened by his appearance. You'll have to be quick and proactive here, explaining how your dog is not a danger.

• Dragging a dog along on a lead seems to be a specialty of the uninitiated, including children. Teach your children to use a treat to lure the puppy when he decides he's walked far enough. If the child still can't get him to move, have her ask for adult help. While it's tempting to give the dog those leftover baked beans from your plate, doing so will only encourage the dog to beg for (and then demand) table feeding. Prevent the problem before it starts.

• Children may become so attached to the puppy that they want to be with him all the time. Teach your child that puppies need time to sleep, think, and dream about the universe. When a puppy walks away from a child, he is saying, "Thanks, I've had enough of you for the moment." Continuing to elicit play after a dog has turned his back is asking for trouble.

• Hugging a dog means affection to us. For a dog, it's a dominant, smothering action they may accept from an adult but not from a child. Ask your children to stroke the dog gently on the chest instead.

C h a p t e r

PREPARING
for Your Bulldog

I t's relatively easy to make the decision that a Bulldog is just right for you. It's much more difficult to find one. (Never buy a dog as a present for someone else. People need to make their own decisions about this critical matter.)

In the first part of this chapter, I'll suggest several options for finding the perfect Bulldog for you. Later in the chapter, I'll talk about how to get ready for his arrival.

FINDING A BULLDOG

Here is my best advice on finding the right Bulldog for you. No matter what your source, don't get a dog with whom you feel uncomfortable. It's your money and your heart. Speaking of money, you'll discover that Bulldog puppies are pricey. About 90% of Bulldog puppies are born by caesarean section. (In the cases of those who aren't, it's usually an accident.) Obviously, this adds to the cost. Litters are often rather small, too, which raises the price.

Puppies are exceptionally charming, but they are not right for everyone. They need much more supervision, attention, and of course, training, than an adult dog. Because they are an independent breed, Bulldogs can take much longer (and require much more patience) to train than a puppy. In a way, a puppy is a bit of a gamble, while the older dog is a better known commodity. And practically speaking, you'll probably have to wait longer to obtain the perfect puppy.

That being said, there is something special about raising your own Bulldog puppy. A well-bred dog raised correctly has a degree of confidence and sense of self-worth that can be harder to find in an adult dog who has been raised by someone else.

The truth of the matter is that great dogs can be acquired at any age—

including those who have reached their senior years. Your own circumstances and inclinations are your best guides.

Breeders

Breeder Pros and Cons

The best source for a high-quality Bulldog, one whom you might want to show, is a responsible breeder who specialises in Bulldogs. However, the truth is that really good Bulldog breeders don't live in every town (or even in every county), so you'll have to do your research. It's well worth it, though.

One of the great things about breeders is that you often have a chance to observe all of the dogs in the litter with their mother. The sire may not be on the premises, but remember that each parent contributes half of the genes! If the sire is not present, the breeder should have some photos of him, at least, and tell you some reasons

One of the advantages to purchasing a Bulldog from a breeder is that you may be able to observe the mother of the puppies.

why she selected him as the sire for her litter. The puppy may resemble one parent more than another, resemble both equally, or look like neither of them. But he should look like a Bulldog!

The only downside to getting your Bulldog through a responsible breeder (aside from finding one) is the waiting you'll probably have to do for your puppy. Most responsible breeders have long waiting lists, and so they have no need to advertise in the newspaper or telephone book. What's the best way to find one, then? The best way to find a responsible breeder in your area is to contact the secretary of your local Bulldog club, who may be able to direct you to a member who is planning a litter. When talking with the secretary, ask when the next shows are and plan to be there. To find your local Bulldog club, go to the Kennel Club's website at www.the-kennel-club.org.uk.

Selecting a Breeder

You may have to travel to find a good breeder, and you almost certainly will have to wait (often for more than a year), but it's worth it. One place you can try is dog shows. Even if you don't plan to show your dog, a show is a great place to see what a show-quality Bulldog looks like. You may also get a chance to speak to breeders, some of whom may be expecting a litter. The world of dog shows is pretty mysterious, but go anyway. This is especially important if you think you might like to show your dog someday. If you find a Bulldog you think is particularly handsome, ask his handler or breeder if there's an upcoming litter or dogs from related lines. Don't do this right before a class, however, because people tend to be a little tense then. Approach your target after the classes have been judged. I always start with a compliment to the dog in question. Most breeders are happy to talk with serious students of the breed. If you encounter someone who is rude, chalk it up to "bad breeding" and talk to a more amiable person.

Curiously enough, often the best choice of breeder is the so-called hobby breeder. A hobby breeder is no rank amateur but someone who breeds for the love of the breed rather than for financial gain. This type of breeder doesn't depend on selling Bulldogs to make a living (as opposed to a commercial breeder). She probably takes her dogs to shows because she is proud of them and of her role in producing them. This breeder enjoys breeding a litter occasionally and is interested in improving her line of

A breeder's puppies should be healthy, friendly, and active.

Bulldogs. Selling to the highest bidder isn't important. You won't see dozens and dozens of dogs locked up in a pen in the garden. A good hobby breeder has made her dogs part of the family, and these pups will easily become part of yours.

After You've Found Your Breeder

Once you find a breeder, expect to be grilled. Bulldog breeders are very particular about the homes their puppies may go to. Their questions may seem intrusive, but breeders are only looking out for the best interests of their puppies. It means they care, and you will benefit from that caring when you bring home your healthy, well-socialised puppy!

You should have some questions for the breeder as well. If you're not planning to show the dog, explain to the breeder that you are looking for a "pet-quality" Bulldog. This doesn't mean there will be anything at all wrong with the puppy. It just means that in the breeder's opinion, the puppy will not achieve a championship in the show ring. Eyes that are too light, a nose that is the wrong colour, or a tail at the incorrect angle are just a few

unimportant factors that may limit a dog's "show worthiness" but will have no effect whatsoever on his ability to make a great pet.

Although some people are adamant that they want a "pet-quality" or a "show-quality" puppy, the truth is that it is often very hard to tell at a young age how the dog will turn out. Many a promising pup has flunked out in the show ring, while occasionally a dog sold as pet-quality unexpectedly blooms and turns into a show champion, much to the surprise of his confused owners. To my way of thinking, the first concern should be getting a healthy, sweet-dispositioned dog whose ancestors are of good stock. Of course he should look nice, too, but as mentioned earlier, you can't tell too much when a puppy is only eight weeks old. At that stage, they're *all* cute. It's also possible that if a show-quality pup strikes your fancy, the breeder will offer to co-own him with you. In most cases, this means that the breeder makes the arrangements to show him, while you can still keep him as a pet most of the time. Don't accept this option without carefully reading over the contract and finding out what is expected of you, though.

Questions to Ask the Breeder

A first-rate breeder will be honest about the shortcomings as well as the glories of Bulldogs, as no breed is perfect in every way. A good breeder can also provide references from previous

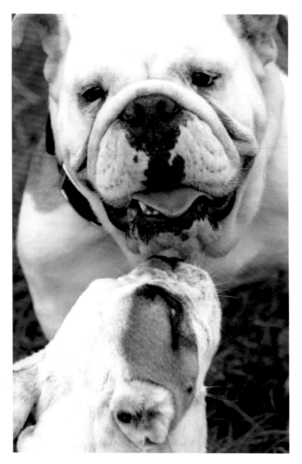

The temperament of the mother is a good indication of what the puppy will be like.

customers. It's a good idea to call these people and ask questions about the health and temperament of the Bulldog they purchased. A breeder who's unwilling to supply references may have something to hide. A good breeder will also agree to take the dog back at any time if you can no longer keep him. If a breeder doesn't have the type of puppy you are looking for, she should be able to direct you to someone else. Breeders who don't seem to know or like any other breeders raise red flags.

Unfortunately, not everyone who shows dogs is well-informed or even cares about important health and temperament issues. Some people want to raise dogs who look good in the show ring, but they don't seem to care if the dogs they raise suffer orthopaedic problems later in life or even die prematurely from inherited disease. Because Bulldogs are subject to certain inherited eye diseases, ask what visual screenings, if any, have been done. Progressive retinal atrophy (PRA), for example, is a screenable health problem. In this disease, the light-sensitive cells in the retina receive an inadequate blood supply. Dogs with this condition first lose night vision, then day vision.

Bulldog Rescue and Rehoming

Bulldog Rescue and Rehoming is the only official service in Great Britain for this breed. Based in West Sussex, they cover the whole of mainland UK using a network of volunteers and foster homes. The organisation takes every precaution to ensure that when a Bulldog needs a new home it is the right one for him.

Their goals are as follows:

- To promote responsible dog ownership amongst those that own a purebred dog.
- To ensure that all those who can no longer keep their Bulldog, have the option of safely placing their dog in a vetted home.
- To find a place of safety for all Bulldogs whose owners can no longer cope or look after their dog properly.
- To offer unbiased breed advice to all those that own a purebred Bulldog.
- To educate Bulldog owners in the hope that Bulldogs in the future can be free from cruelty, abuse and neglect.

There is no treatment, and the disease always affects both eyes. However, it develops rather slowly, giving the dog time to become used to the condition. The Kennel Club and the British Veterinary Association (BVA) offer breeders the chance to eye test to screen for any possible eye problems. See The Kennel Club website for more details. Another problem in modern dogs is hip dysplasia, a condition in which the thighbone does not fit correctly into the hip socket. This condition is extremely common in Bulldogs. A similar condition of the front limbs, elbow dysplasia, is also common. There is a test available to screen the parent dogs for these problems, but many Bulldog breeders fail to use it, first because anaesthesia is required for the test (and Bulldogs are highly sensitive to anaesthesia) and also because most Bulldogs fail the test.

Reliable rescue centres are committed to finding safe, forever homes for their dogs.

One shortcut I have used to sort out good breeders from bad ones is to ask the simple question, "What are the goals of your breeding programme?" If the breeder stares at you blankly, you may want to reconsider buying a dog from her. A responsible breeder, however, will not stop talking about it once you broach the topic. Ask the breeder how long she has been breeding dogs. Although every breeder has to begin at some point, inexperienced buyers are best matched with experienced breeders. You should also ask the breeder how often she breeds Bulldogs. Breeders with large numbers of litters over a short period are suspect. Other

Don't let the breeder tell you that she will send you the papers later. You are entitled to them immediately.

questions you may want to consider include:

- What organisations does she belong to, and does she participate in conformation or other activities with her dogs?
- Will she show you the puppies' health certificates?
- What are the strengths and weaknesses of her line?

Finally, be sure to inquire about anything in the contract that you do not understand.

Rescue Centres and Shelters

Rescue and Shelter Pros and Cons

Breeders are not your only option for Bulldog acquisition. Believe it or not, hundreds of Bulldogs are lost, abandoned, or given to shelters and rescue centres every year. The reason is not hard to find. People acquire these wonderful dogs without understanding their special needs. They then decide that the Bulldog is too much trouble or not right for their lifestyle, so the dog joins the ranks of thousands of other dogs and cats in the same boat.

Most rescue Bulldogs are four or five years old, and some have health or behavioural problems that led their owners to surrender them to shelters or rescue organisations. Some have problems with aggression, some aren't suitable for children, and others have housetraining issues. While taking in a rescue dog is tremendously satisfying emotionally, it's only truthful to say that it can be hard work, too. After all, you won't be able to show such an animal; he may have phobias, medical problems, or bad habits. Yet this can also be true of even the most well-bred dog. He may also be a much older dog than you planned on having. And although he will certainly be less expensive than a dog from a reputable breeder, you'll end up spending just as much money on him in short order—more if you decide to take in a dog with special medical needs. So why would you possibly even entertain such an idea in the first place?

One important reason is that adopting a dog from a shelter or rescue centre makes a real, tangible difference in more lives than you can imagine. First of all, every shelter, every pound, and every rescue group in the country is full. Every day, thousands of dogs are put to sleep, not because they are ill or vicious, but because there is simply no more room for them. Few dogs who go to the

shelter will find homes, and around twenty-one dogs a day are put to sleep. Rescue groups have better success, but most are too small to take in large numbers of dogs. When you accept a shelter or rescue dog into your home, you are making room for another dog who may now have a chance at life. You've saved two dogs!

The difference you'll make in your new dog's life is immeasurable. You may be providing your rescue dog's first toy, bed, and love. You may be taking him for his first walk, his first romp, his first visit. You may be giving him the first kind words he's ever heard. However, the biggest difference will be in your own life. The feeling of knowing you saved a life will enrich your own. The love you get from a previously unloved and unwanted dog easily matches any puppy devotion. Bulldogs in particular have loyalty to spare; your new dog will not "pine away" for his former owners, most of whom neglected him. He will transfer his abiding affection to you. Even elderly dogs make excellent pets, usually giving remarkably little trouble. Most of them are happy to live out their last few years in peace, sunning themselves in the garden and going for walks down the street. I have an elderly friend who recently adopted a senior female dog, saying happily, "We can be old ladies together."

The best Bulldog puppy is one who is friendly without being aggressive.

Selecting a Rescue Centre or Shelter

Some rescue centres and shelters are responsible and some are not, just as with every other source for finding a Bulldog. Choosing a rescue centre that is associated with a national Bulldog club is a good option, if you can find one near you. Ask for references or the names of others who have adopted from the rescue centre.

Just as you would probably have to wait for a Bulldog puppy from a breeder, you may have to wait for a rescue also. This will depend on the availability of the dog, your willingness to travel, and your specific needs. Some people manage to get their rescue dog in just a couple of weeks. Others have waited five years.

A reliable rescue centre issues a contract the same way a good breeder does. Nearly all rescue groups stipulate that if the dog doesn't suit or can't adapt to your family, you will return him to the rescue centre, not resell him or give him away. Most rescue centres also require a home visit and vet check before they will allow you to adopt one of their dogs. The dogs they deal with have already been severely traumatised; rescue groups want to make sure that the new home will be the last one.

Questions to Ask the Rescue Centre or Shelter

Be diligent in asking the rescue centre or shelter relevant questions about the dog's age, health, and temperament. Find out how the dog ended up in the shelter. If he was given up by his former owner, ask if you can contact this person. Chances are that you won't be able to, but it never hurts to ask.

Bulldog puppies should look clean and healthy.

The truth is that no rescue centre or shelter can give you an iron-clad guarantee about their charges. However, a good shelter or rescue centre will take the dog back readily if he proves not to be a

Good Bulldog owners are first of all good citizens. Don't consider a Bulldog if your lease agreement doesn't allow you to have a pet.

If you do have permission to get a dog, comply with all regulations regarding dog identification and vaccinations. Be aware that you are responsible for where your dog poops, and be prepared to pick it up!

Remember, if your Bulldog is off your property, he needs to be on a lead. While he is not likely to go charging off on a trek into the wilderness, he can get into trouble remarkably quickly. Play it safe.

good fit in your home.

CHOOSING THE RIGHT BULLDOG FOR YOU

Physical Appearance

The eyes and ears of the Bulldog puppy should be clear and free of discharge, and the coat should have a clean, healthy appearance. The gums should be a healthy pink colour, not pale or red. The puppy should exude that delicious "puppy scent." Puppies with swollen tummies might have a severe roundworm (*Toxocara canis*) infestation. Nearly all puppies are born with a case of roundworms, but this problem should be resolved by the time you are ready to choose your puppy. Of course, you will make arrangements for the puppy to see your own veterinarian immediately for a general checkup to make sure that everything is in good order. In male puppies, both testicles should be descended into the scrotum. Dogs with only one descended testicle should be avoided. If you can't tell, ask your vet to check for you.

While looking at the litter of puppies, take some time to examine the dam (and sire, if present) also. These animals are the surest indication of what your puppy will look like when he reaches maturity.

If you are adopting or purchasing an adult Bulldog, ask

permission to take him to your veterinarian for a thorough physical checkup before you sign the contract. A good rescue centre will insist you do. Also be sure to ask for all veterinary records.

Temperament

Looks are not the only important thing to consider when selecting a Bulldog puppy. Temperament, including aggression and shyness, is largely inherited, so make sure the dam is friendly, mild, and outgoing, assuming these are qualities you want in your own puppy.

Choose a puppy who is friendly without being aggressive. A shy or retiring puppy may be ill or too reserved to make a good family pet, but a more reserved puppy may be just the choice for a quiet single person. Regardless of your personality, it's very possible that you will find a puppy or dog whose personality perfectly matches yours. Choosing the right puppy ultimately depends more on intuition than on logic. I always feel that when you see the right puppy, you'll just know it.

It's also a good idea to perform a little sociability test with your puppy prospect. He should follow you happily, and when you kneel down and call him, he should toddle over to you eagerly and not fear eye contact. If a puppy seems unduly frightened of a noise that is not terribly loud (pills shaken in a bottle, jangling change), he may not be secure.

The adult Bulldog should have many of these same characteristics. Overall, he should be friendly and confident, with no trace of viciousness or shyness.

The Show Dog

If you're in the market for a show dog, it's important to find a show breeder who will work with you and mentor you. To improve your chances of getting a show quality dog, you may have to settle for an older puppy (five to eight months old) who will give better indications of what he'll be like at maturity than an eight-week-old will. But remember that nothing is guaranteed. Be prepared to love and adore your Bulldog whether or not he turns out to be "show quality." You know he's the most beautiful dog on earth, and that's what counts.

Sometimes a breeder may offer you an older puppy or young adult dog who may not have "worked out" in the show ring. Don't overlook this opportunity for getting a very nice dog at a lower

Accredited Breeder Scheme

This voluntary scheme, which was launched in 2004 by The Kennel Club, was set up to promote good breeding practices. The Scheme helps to ensure that prospective owners have all the information they need to find a healthy and well adjusted puppy. While this is a good place to start looking for your puppy, breed clubs and societies are also a good source of information.

cost. An older Bulldog will bond to your entire family quickly. The same is true, of course, of a rescue dog.

Overall, it's important to spend plenty of time with the litter. You may even want to return in a day or two to look again. A good breeder will not hurry you or pressure you into buying a certain puppy. On the other hand, it's possible that the puppy you have your eye on will be sold out from under you unless you put down a deposit or make special arrangements with the breeder.

PAPERWORK

One bit of paperwork that comes with a purebred Bulldog is a pedigree, which is really just a family tree of your dog. If you live in the United Kingdom, be sure to ask if the dog is being sold on a Bulldog Breed Council Puppy Contract.

If you buy a Bulldog from a reputable breeder who has registered the parents with the Kennel Club, you will probably be eligible to register your dog with the Kennel Club. Some breeders sell pets on a limited registration basis, meaning that the pet has to be neutered but can still be registered. Registered purebred dogs are eligible to compete in KC sponsored events like obedience competition and agility trials. Your dog also gets to have an official registered name that is unique. If you register your puppy with the Kennel Club you can get six weeks of free pet health insurance. The breeder should register the litter with the Kennel Club (assuming the litter is eligible), then provide you with transfer of ownership papers with everything signed and ready for you to send in. When you send in this paperwork, ownership is transferred to you and the pupy is officially registered.

You should also receive some written care instructions, including the kind of food the puppy is accustomed to eating and how much and how often. In most cases, the breeder will give you a supply of the food to tide you over until you can buy some yourself. You may also receive a favourite toy or some of the bedding the puppy is used to.

A breeder will also supply a sales contract that includes the

terms under which the puppy is sold.

BRINGING YOUR BULLDOG HOME

Now that you've purchased or adopted your dog, it's time to bring him home!

Timing

Timing your Bulldog acquisition properly is very important. For most people, acquiring a dog during the holidays is a bad idea. With so much going on and so many visitors tramping in and out, a holiday can be a bewildering time for new dogs and new owners. It's usually best to wait until things settle down. However, for some people, holidays are perfect. Teachers, for example, often have time off from classes and thus find themselves with more time to work with a new dog. Still, if it's the dead of winter and you live in a rural area, it might be a good idea to refrain from getting a dog

Your new puppy will feel more secure if you allow him to sleep in your bedroom with you.

until the spring. Nobody wants to attempt housetraining during a wet, muddy winter, including your puppy.

Remember that although this is a thrilling day for you, your new puppy may not be so happy about the experience. From his point of view, he's been dognapped from the only home he's ever known, put in a car where he might have gotten sick, and brought to a new, strange-smelling place with people and possibly other pets he's never seen before. Don't blame him if he's not as overjoyed as you'd like him to be. He misses his mother, littermates, and former family. On the other hand, Bulldogs are good-natured and adaptable. He will quickly bond to your family.

The First Night

If your new Bulldog is a puppy, he'll need plenty of sleep. It's easy for overexcited family members to "overplay" the puppy, but if you remember that he's much like a human baby who needs his beauty rest, you'll have a happier Bulldog.

Both adults and puppies may experience distress at having left their previous home. This is normal. Keep to your dog's former routine as much as possible to lessen the shock, and provide plenty of comfort and support. Schedule and routine is very important. Feed at the same time and place every day. He'll soon regard your home as his own.

Give your Bulldog his own special spot in the house. The spot will be where his crate is set up. If you don't choose to use a crate, you can still have a special spot with the dog's blanket, bed, and toys. This will be his private retreat, the spot to which he can retire to when things get rough at home. Never use this space as punishment.

The first night is bound to be traumatic. There's a lot of noise and confusion, and he's just been put in a strange room and left alone in the dark. Why shouldn't he cry? The solution is so easy. Simply allow your new puppy to sleep in the bedroom with you, in his own bed by your side. There is no need to terrorise him by forcing him to sleep alone in a distant part of the house. Furthermore, it will ease your housetraining chores considerably if you are close to your puppy. When you sense he's beginning to stir, you can jump right up and head outside with him into the cold night.

Having your puppy sleep with you in your bedroom will not

Wriggly Puppy
Don't allow young children to carry the puppy. Even a careful child can drop a wriggly dog, and your puppy could be seriously injured or frightened. Let them hold the puppy in their arms while they are seated, preferably on the ground.

Spay and Neuter

Puppies can actually be safely spayed or neutered when they are only a few weeks old, and this is a plan many shelters follow to help curb the pet overpopulation. Some people even think it's better to do it at this age, since young puppies heal so fast. Most veterinarians still prefer to wait a bit longer, however, as they believe the surgery is easier. Some also believe it's better for the puppy to mature before neutering.

"spoil him." It will not make him vicious. It will not turn him into an uncontrollable alpha dog. It will simply make him aware that you are his parent and you will be there to comfort him the way his own mother did before you. Some people allow their dogs to sleep in the bed with them, and if you are entertaining this idea, you can start him right off snuggled by your pillow. This will make your dog more, not less, secure. However, because I strongly advise that you crate train your puppy, it may be best to allow him to sleep by your side in his own crate. That way he won't fall off the bed or wander around the house and get into trouble.

If your puppy cries during the night, talk to him quietly (tell him a few jokes) until he falls asleep. Make sure he is warm. He may wake up a time or two during the night, but this is normal. He'll soon sleep contentedly throughout the night.

SPAYING AND NEUTERING

Unless you are planning to show your puppy, there is no reason not to neuter or spay him or her.

Neutering or spaying offers many advantages:
- Reduces aggressive behaviour
- Lessens the tendency to wander
- Eliminates or drastically reduces "marking" in males
- Practically eliminates the possibility of uterine infections and cancers, ovarian cancer, and prostate and testicular cancers.

The procedure is really a very simple one, and terrific new anaesthetics let your dog wake up sooner after the surgery, without that "anaesthesia hangover." This is important for Bulldogs, many of whom have trouble with anaesthesia. Because the surgery doesn't involve cutting into muscle, dogs recover quite quickly (just a day or so), with very little pain. To receive the optimal health results from spaying your female, have it done before the first heat cycle, which occurs at five to six months of age. This will vastly reduce the chances of mammary cancer. If you wait until your dog goes through three to four heat cycles, there is no reduction in cancer risk.

Don't give your dog any food or water the night before the neutering or spaying (he or she might get sick), and give him or her a few days to recover afterward. Your Bulldog will be ready to eat and drink small amounts several hours after coming home from the surgery.

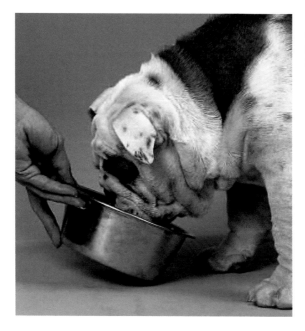

Sturdy, stainless steel food and water dishes are hard to break and easy to clean.

BULLDOG BELONGINGS

Your Bulldog will give you all of the love, loyalty, and laughs a person could ever want—all that you need to do is to provide him with the simple things he needs. The first need, of course, is love. And while I know you love your Bulldog, you have to let him in on the secret! Plenty of attention, hugs, quality time, and just hanging out together will fill the bill very nicely. Bulldogs aren't keen on long-distance love, so you may need to adjust your schedule a bit to humour him.

Food and Water

Canine Nutrition

While I talk about this in detail later, remember that your Bulldog requires a high-quality, nutritionally balanced diet. This includes open access to clean, fresh water. If you need to change his diet, do so gradually so as not to cause gastrointestinal upset.

Your Bulldog puppy will initially consume puppy food, but when he is about eight months old, you can gradually begin switching to a high-quality adult food. Feed the best food you can find. If it seems expensive, look at it this way: A less expensive dog food is lower in essential nutrients than the better

back, which makes walking a breeze. I strongly recommend this harness for Bulldogs.

Lead

You should also have a regular 4- to 6-foot (1 to 2 m) lead made of leather, waxed cotton, or nylon. Chain leads are noisy, heavy, and unnecessary. They give no warning when they are about to break, and they can develop sharp edges. Good leather leads are durable and comfortable, especially as they age. Beware of cheap leather leads, however, which can be rough on your hands. The downside of leather leads is that they are slow to dry out once they get wet. They are also attractive to dogs' taste buds. Never let your Bulldog take the lead in his mouth. Once he gets a taste for it, you're doomed. (Some owners spray their leather leads with a bitter apple spray or a similar aversive product to discourage chewing.)

Teach your puppy to accept the lead by leaving a short one on him for a while. Supervise him the entire time so that he doesn't catch the lead on anything or chew it to pieces. He will probably fuss with it a bit at first, but he'll soon get used it. When you do pick up the end, follow him for a while. When you take the lead yourself, call the puppy to you gently; when he toddles up to you, give him a treat and praise him. Very soon he will be happily following you everywhere. At this stage, try not to struggle with your puppy. If he resists, don't tug the other way, but don't give in either. Lure him to you with a biscuit. He'll soon catch on that it's fun to do what he's asked. Keep puppy lessons short—five minutes a couple of times a day is enough.

A crate is an invaluable housetraining tool.

Pooper-Scooper

As a good citizen, you'll want to keep your garden and neighbourhood clean. The advantage of a pooper-scooper is that it saves your back and keeps your nose distant from the object you are picking up. On the other hand, a pooper-scooper is never around at the right time, and it's silly to carry one

A baby gate will prevent your Bulldog from wandering into areas of the house that may contain dangerous items.

on a walk. You can purchase sturdy little baggie pooper-scoopers at any pet shop, but a plain old sandwich bag works about as well and is much cheaper.

Bed

Your Bulldog needs his own bed in his own special place. Choose a sturdy bed that is resistant to chewing. The bedding can be made of any soft, washable material; the "sheepskin" kind is often favoured. However, plain old towels or an unwashed t-shirt that carries your scent will work too. A wicker basket is a bad choice for a puppy bed, as it is so attractive to some puppies that they will begin to devour it. Wicker can break off into sharp fragments that can lodge in or pierce your puppy's oesophagus, tummy, or intestines. There is an allergy-free bedding that is available from pet shops which is made from pure fibres to protect your dog from dust mites and keep away the bacteria and allergens that may irritate.

Crate

A wire mesh crate is an important housetraining tool and general purpose den for your dog. Even though real wolves only den up to have cubs, domestic dogs appreciate the value of their own place if they are introduced to it carefully. Dogs should be crated when travelling and may need to recuperate after surgery, so it's a good idea to get your dog accustomed to it now. While fibreglass kennels are available, your Bulldog really requires something with better air ventilation.

If you're using a crate for housetraining purposes, a large crate may be too big, as it offers extra space in which the Bulldog can relieve himself. Many large crates can be sectioned off with removable panels to accommodate him as he grows.

Exercise Pen

The so-called x-pen or puppy pen is a portable wire playpen for your dog. It's great for travel or when you need to confine your dog to a specific area of the house. While you are cooking dinner or cleaning the oven, for example, your puppy can watch you safely. Even more important, you can keep an eye on him. Watch for those telltale squirming signs, and you can use the x-pen as a housetraining tool as well as a containment device.

Doggie Doors

Although not practical for every household, a doggie door opening into a fenced garden makes life easier for everyone involved. The door even acts as a housetraining aid by letting your Bulldog come and go as he likes. They install in most wood or composite doors in minutes. The easiest ones for dogs to use have just a clear, flexible plastic panel, but you can also purchase high-tech models that you can adjust mechanically, which will allow you to prevent the dog from going out or coming in.

Baby Gates

One thing you don't want is your precious puppy wandering all around

the house unsupervised. Because you will need to block off certain rooms and the stairway, you should choose a baby gate that's approved by consumer organisations. You can purchase some made especially for dogs. However, if your dog is a major chewer, don't get a wooden gate.

Toys

Proper toys for Bulldogs need to be big—too big to swallow! Remember what a big head your dog has. Small balls, rawhide strips, cow hooves, and similarly-sized treats can be deadly. Because of the Bulldog's unusual bite, he can't chew very efficiently. Bulldogs can choke to death on bones and balls more easily than many other breeds. Refrain from giving your dog battery-powered toys, because they can kill if ingested. If you must use such a toy, supervise your dog constantly. However, avoidance is best.

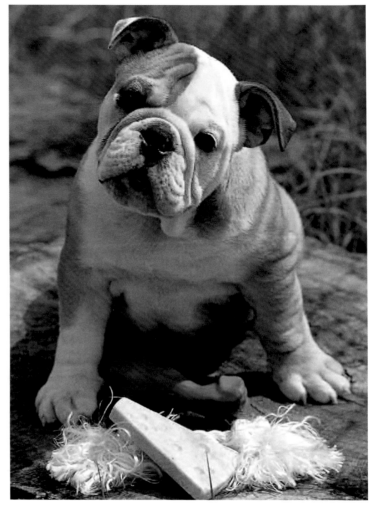

Provide your Bulldog with safe toys that are too big for him to swallow.

Select safe toys with parts that won't detach and get swallowed. As far as toy material goes, each one provides a special experience for your Bulldog. Rubber toys give the best jaw and mouth exercise; they're ideal for chewers and dogs who spend a lot of time alone. (Some of these are hollow, so you can hide little treats in there.) These toys are also good for playing games with your dog. Vinyl toys usually contain squeakers that dogs love, but they're not very sturdy for aggressive chewers. Cloth toys are comforting to dogs, partly because they become saturated with the dog's own scent. This is probably the kind of toy that your dog will

adopt for his very "own." Rope toys are excellent for tug-of-war games. The flavoured kinds are also good for chewing, and the fibres often work to keep teeth and gums in shape. While many dogs enjoy rawhide chips and bones, I don't recommend them as Bulldog toys; they can be too easily swallowed and cause injury. Nylon bones, like Nylabones, help keep teeth clean and healthy. The new flavoured varieties are especially appealing to dogs.

Don't overstock your dog's toy supply at first. Overabundance can lead to boredom as surely as insufficiency creates destructiveness. The main purpose of toys, from your point of view at least, is to distract the dog from appealing items like your expensive shoes and wallet. Before the toy gets chewed down to swallowable size, toss it away. A new toy is a lot cheaper than a broken heart.

Cleaning Supplies

Non-ammonia-based cleaners and carpet deodorisers are all handy to have on hand, as are plenty of paper towels.

Grooming Supplies

You'll need the following grooming supplies to keep your

A nail grinder or pair of nail clippers is an essential grooming tool.

Bulldog clean and healthy. (See Chapter 5 for more detailed information.)

- Brushes
- Shampoo
- Cotton-tip applicators and cotton balls
- Baby powder
- Mustard squirt bottle (clean and empty, of course) to squirt cleaner into the hard-to-access wrinkles, especially under the nose rope
- Nail clippers or a grinder
- Canine toothbrush and toothpaste
- Grooming table (while not a necessity, it may come in handy)

Luckily, Bulldog puppies don't require a whole lot of grooming until they shed their first coat, but it's a great idea to get them used to the process.

Medical Supplies

The following items, many found right in your medicine cabinet, will be helpful to have on hand. (See Chapter 8 for a complete first-aid kit list.)

- Peroxide
- Antibiotic cream
- Rectal thermometer
- Visine for eye irritation
- Benadryl in case of insect bite or sting
- Petroleum jelly
- Lemon juice
- First-aid booklet for dogs

Clean Toys

Clean your dog's rubber and plastic toys once a week in hot, soapy water, and throw soft toys in the washing machine. Dirty, slimy balls and rubber or nylon bones are neither pleasant to behold nor healthy for your dog.

Identification

To protect your new friend, you should make sure he carries ID at all times. No matter what additional kinds of identification you may use, outfit your dog with a flat collar and tag that carries *your* name, address, and telephone number. You can also put the information right on some kinds of collars with a simple laundry marker, so your dog can be identified even if the tags are somehow ripped off.

The latest technology allows you to microchip your Bulldog. The microchip cannot get lost, nor can it be altered. The microchip is only the size of a grain of rice, encapsulated in a special

biocompatible material that allows your dog to wear it safely under his skin. Your veterinarian will implant it between the shoulder blades. (The dog does not have to undergo anaesthesia for the process—it is quick and painless.) Once implanted, the microchip is there for good, with no batteries required. These microchips have an estimated lifespan of 25 years and so will undoubtedly outlive your dog. The number of the microchip is entered into a central database, which allows you to notify the company if you move or if the dog's ownership has changed.

If your dog gets lost, veterinarians, dog wardens, or rescue centre personnel have handheld scanners that can be passed over the dog. If a microchip is present, its number will be displayed on the scanner. Of course, not everyone who finds a lost dog has a scanner or knows enough to take the animal to a vet or rescue centre that does. Therefore, the microchip does not replace traditional ID tags!

Disaster Kit

In addition to your first-aid kit, be prepared for a major disaster, whether it be weather-related or something else. Here's what your dog needs:

- Food (two-week supply—dry food should be placed in airtight containers and rotated every three months)
- Water (two-week supply—rotate every two months; figure that you will need 2 pints of water per day)
- Blanket and towels
- Carrier or crate
- Muzzle or gauze and tape to make one
- Medications, contact information, and vet records
- Food bowls
- Extra collars and leads with ID on each
- Grooming supplies
- Toys and chews
- Hot water bottle
- Thick gloves
- Paper towels
- Disinfectant

• Life preserver for dog if you're in a flood area

It is very important to have proof of ownership of your pet in case of a dispute. Make copies of your dog's registration, adoption papers, shelter release, proofs of purchase, and microchip/tattoo or other identification information. Some people have even spray painted their phone number on their dog in case of a widespread disaster. Put the ID information in the evacuation kit as well, along with a list of each of your animals and their species/breed, age, sex, colour, and other distinguishing characteristics. Keep current photographs of your animals in the evacuation kit for identification purposes. Include yourself in some of the photos to help establish your claim to your pet.

You should always have a disaster plan for each kind of foreseeable disaster, including a good evacuation place. Keep a list of nearby hotels that allow pets. You can even ask if a hotel that normally has a no-pet policy will waive that requirement in case of an emergency. A list of boarding facilities may also be an option.

Try as much as possible to take your pet with you—you may not be able to return to claim him. If you can't take your pet, or if he is alone when the disaster hits, prepare by keeping a notice permanently on the front door as to the number of pets inside so that rescuers or kindly neighbours may be able to help remove them. Keep extra leads and collars in a box near the door to help get your animals out safely.

PUPPY-PROOFING YOUR HOME

Indoors

Your house is a thrilling montage of dangerous, expensive, and sentimentally irreplaceable items. Your Bulldog will eat, chew, rip up, or urinate on every one of them unless you take proper precautions. Some vets keep files of bizarre items their patients have devoured. I knew a dog who swallowed a 3-foot (1m) necktie (and amazingly passed it). Other swallowed materials have included mobile phones, knives, tinsel, dominoes, nails, thermometers, dental radiographs, and a host of other things.

Puppies are drawn to electrical cables, poisonous plants, antifreeze, and human medications. If you have even the slightest doubt, lock it up, barricade it, or watch the puppy like a hawk when he's in the room with it.

What's in a Name?

Although it probably doesn't matter a whole lot what you name your Bulldog, a few simple rules should apply. If you have more than one dog, their names should be different enough that they (and you) can easily tell them apart. The best names are usually simple ones consisting of one or two syllables (although I confess to owning one dog named Tammy Faye Baker-Basset née Russell).

In most ways, your dog doesn't care what you call him, as long as it's not late to dinner. The tone of your voice when you say his name is much more important, and you should only use your dog's name in conjunction with a happy event—not just, "Come here, Otto, so I can give you a bath!" The more pleasant associations a dog has with his name, the more likely he will be to respond to it.

Cupboards

Keep the cupboards locked and put away all household cleaners and medication. (You should never give your dog medications meant for people without approval from your veterinarian, and that includes aspirin.) Use child safety latches for cupboards that your dog can reach.

Rubbish

Keep the rubbish bin under the sink or in another inaccessible place. (I keep mine behind the cellar door.) Once dogs start stealing rubbish, they don't quit, and it's practically impossible to train them out of it. It's much simpler and smarter to manage the problem rather than try vainly to solve it.

Stairways

Close off dangerous stairways. It's bad for a puppy to go bouncing up and down stairs anyway, and you certainly don't want him out of your sight. Excellent baby and pet gates are made for this purpose.

Electrical Cables

Put up loose electrical cables, or at least tape them to the skirting board where they will be less conspicuous.

Houseplants

Many common houseplants are toxic to pets. And even though a grown dog might not be tempted, puppies are oral creatures who test everything in their mouths. Don't leave a puppy unattended, any more than you would a two-year-old child.

Portable Heaters and Fireplaces

Because Bulldogs seek warmth, portable heaters and fireplaces can be lethal for your dog. If you do have a fireplace, use a screen. Put portable heaters out of your Bulldog's reach.

Outdoors

Bulldogs are skillful at getting into

The More the Merrier?

Many people enjoy their Bulldogs so much that they are tempted to get another one or two. Multiple Bulldogs are twice as fun as one. However, there's no question that adding another dog means more expense and more time. There's something very special about the relationship between one dog and one person, and the more dogs you add to your home, the less attention each dog will receive.

In some cases, people get a puppy when their first dog starts to age. Sometimes the new addition may revive the older dog, but in other cases, the puppy will only annoy and stress the older dog, who may feel relegated to the background. In worst-case scenarios, inter-dog aggression can develop, although this is usually mild and temporary. And the problem with getting two puppies is that you'll end up with two very old dogs at the same time. If you would like to get a second Bulldog puppy, it may be best to wait until the first one is two or three years old. Of course, you can get a suitable rescue dog at any time.

Only you can decide how many dogs are right for your family and how many you can handle. Be honest with yourself before you get another dog, and ask yourself why you need or want one. People who are involved with rescue are especially in danger of overloading on dogs, thinking, "If I don't adopt them, who will?" In worst-case scenarios, this can lead to animal-hoarding, which is a recognised mental disorder (and notoriously hard to cure).

trouble outside the house as well as inside. Some garden items are dangerous, some are valuable, and many are both. To keep your dog and your possessions safe outdoors, fence off areas you don't want him to have access to and pick up toys and rubbish.

Lawn Chemicals

Keep the use of lawn chemicals to a minimum. No chemicals at all is best, as they are dangerous for dogs. You are walking several feet above the treated area, but your poor Bulldog has his nose right in it.

Fencing

Before you bring your puppy home, check out the fence. Bulldogs are capable of digging under fences as well as shoving themselves through weak spots. If there's an outside gate to your fenced garden, padlock it to keep out dangerous or thoughtless children who think it would be fun to let the dog out.

Doghouse

Many dogs enjoy the comfort of their very own doghouse if they spend time in the garden. Bulldogs appreciate the shady retreat it

offers, as long as they're not expected to spend the night there, or worse, are chained to the thing. Consider the doghouse to be the equivalent of your Bully's outdoor crate that he can wander in and out of as the mood strikes him. However, doghouses can trap heat, so they are poor shelters when it is very hot.

Chaining Your Dog

In desperation from allergies or a passionate devotion to a spotless home, some people resort to chaining their pets outside. This is wrong. It creates a lonely, territorial, barking, sad pet. Chains can entangle your dog so that he injures himself or can't reach food and water.

A dog on a chain is deprived of love, training, and attention. Dogs are social creatures meant to share your life. Very few dogs enjoy spending hours alone. They want to be with you, which is wise of them. They belong there.

Having said that, I will concede that there are times when it's necessary to tether (not chain) your dog. The purpose of the tether is to restrict the dog's movements while you're busy planting petunias or babecueing. On these occasions, you will be outside with the dog and glancing at him from time to time to make sure he is not in trouble.

Seasonal Challenges

Changes in the weather require you to make special adjustments for your Bulldog. This rather unnatural breed can't handle many of the harder blows that nature deals out.

Drafts and Chill

Comfort-loving Bulldogs aren't meant to endure bitter temperature extremities. They aren't Huskies. Their very short noses don't even give them a chance to "warm up" freezing air as they suck it into their lungs, making the cold harder on them than on an otherwise similar, long-nosed breed. Keep your dog dry, warm, and away from drafts. Tile and uncarpeted floors can be cold on Bully tootsies, so make sure he has a warm bed to sleep in.

Walking in Winter's Wonderland

If you can convince your Bulldog to accompany you for a winter's stroll, be sure to wipe the snow and ice off his feet on your

return. Many pavements are treated with rock salt or antifreeze, both of which can cause harm to your Bulldog if he licks his feet afterwards. (Be sure to clean between his toes, too—it gets icky in there.)

Dogs can also fall victim to frostbite, just as we can. Their feet, nose, and ears are especially susceptible, and it doesn't take long for them to suffer from exposure. It may not feel that cold to you, but you're bigger (size conserves heat) and more bundled up than your poor Bully. A coat

If you are travelling with your dog, plan ahead to ensure that he is comfortable and safe for the duration of the journey.

helps keep his central body warm, but it won't do much for his extremities. Frostbitten skin is red or grey, and it may peel off. If your Bulldog does happen to get frostbite, apply warm, moist towels to slowly thaw the affected areas. Call your vet for more advice.

Deep snow makes it difficult for a Bulldog to accomplish some of his necessary *toilette*. You may have to dig out a space for him.

Summer Heat

Summer heat is a terrible enemy of the Bulldog. Very few dogs enjoy the heat (they can perspire only through the pads of their feet and noses), and Bulldogs are even less adept than normal dogs at dealing with it. Some actually suffer from permanent chronic airway obstruction! (This condition can be surgically corrected.) Bulldogs must be observed and supervised carefully when they are outside in the summer. They must have good ventilation, and in hot areas, they should have access to air conditioning when the outside temperature climbs above 80°F (27°C). Their crates should be made of wire mesh for best ventilation. To keep your Bully comfortable, get him used to eating ice chips from the time he's a puppy. And of course, always provide shade.

When taking your Bulldog out for a stroll in the summer months, do so in the morning or evening when it's cooler, and if possible, keep him off hot tarmac and concrete. Bring along a collapsible water bowl.

Cats

Bulldogs are peaceable creatures who generally get along fine with cats. The reverse isn't necessarily true, however. Playful puppies can unnerve cats, who may respond with severe stress symptoms such as inappropriate urination. Give the cat plenty of time and space on his own. (Lock up the pup if you need to, and make sure he responds to your directions to "leave it." For more information on this and other training, refer to Chapter 6.) And remember that a cat who has been declawed has no means of protection.

TRAVELLING WITH YOUR BULLDOG

Life is so much more fun if you can take your Bulldog wherever you go. Of course, you will have to obey the rules of common courtesy first. If you're going to stay with friends, ask in advance if your Bulldog is welcome. The same goes for hotels, and campgrounds. Don't just show up without first making sure pets are allowed and finding out what the rules regarding them are. You can find many of these hotels by going to www.dogfriendly.co.uk.

If you are lucky enough to secure a pet-friendly hotel, be considerate of the other guests. Don't allow your dog to mark the furniture, bark his head off, or defecate without you cleaning it up. If you have to leave your Bulldog alone in a hotel room, put a "Do Not Disturb" sign on the door and tell the front desk there is a dog inside. Most hotels require that the animal be crated while in the room, especially if you won't be there.

Always make sure your Bulldog is properly vaccinated for the area in which you are travelling, especially if you are travelling abroad with your Bulldog. Check with your vet to make sure your dog is up-to-date on any shots he may need. Take his vet records and recent photos in case he gets lost.

Also, double-check all identification tags. The tags should include a way to reach you or someone who knows where you are. It doesn't do any good to have the person who located your dog

"Animal Card"

What if you have an accident while away from home? To make sure your pets will receive attention while you're in intensive care, carry an "animal card" in your wallet. This card should contain information about each of your pets, including name, species, location, and special care instructions. It should also give contact information for the person you have arranged to take care of your pet. If you haven't made such arrangements, please do. Even if you get hit by a car, your Bulldog still needs his dinner!

call your home if you aren't going to be there.

It's also a good idea to take a simple first-aid kit with you, including a safe anti-diarrhoea medication. Dogs tend to get diarrhoea on trips either from the excitement or the strange water. You should also bring along important phone numbers, including that of your veterinarian, and a 24-hour emergency veterinary surgery near where you'll be staying.

Travelling by Car

Most Bulldogs enjoy travel by car, but if your dog is not accustomed to it, take him for some practice runs before the big day. Feed him about one third of what you normally would before starting out to reduce the chances of his getting sick. However, bring some extra food or snacks with you.

Put your Bulldog in a crate or safety harness in the back seat. You don't want him to turn into a football flying through the windshield when you brake for a deer. If travelling by car in the summer months, keep your dog cool by putting icepacks in his crate. Make sure the crate is well-ventilated.

Whenever you take your Bulldog out, think, "Hmm…what if my car breaks down on the road?" Be prepared for that happening. Your travel plans should always include bringing along a lead, a supply of drinking water, and a bowl. If you're travelling during the warmer months, bring a cooling vest or towel that can be wetted, a kiddie pool that can be unfolded, and shade netting or a sun shade.

Even if you don't break down, be prepared to stop about once every two hours. And of course, you should never leave your Bulldog in a hot car, not even for a few minutes. Temperatures can soar to 120°F (49°C) in a closed car even with the windows partway open. Temperatures below freezing are also dangerous for your Bulldog. In addition, under no circumstances should you permit your Bulldog to ride with his mug hanging outside the car windows, charming as the sight might be to fellow drivers. First, you might cause an accident. Even worse, debris or other particles can get into your dog's eyes, injuring or infecting them.

Carsickness

While most Bulldogs love to travel, some don't and experience carsickness. In a few instances, carsickness has a physical basis,

Travel Checklist

If you need to take your Bulldog on the road with you, be prepared.

Make sure your hotel or campsite allows dogs and call ahead to confirm the booking.

Be courteous and respectful to others, this includes cleaning up after your dog.

Don't forget the lead, collar and identification tags.

Take food and water bowls and a supply of your dog's regular food.

Always use a crate or a doggy seatbelt when travelling by car.

Chew toys and other comforting items in your dog's crate will help him feel more secure.

usually a problem in the inner ear, which can often be safely remedied with an over-the-counter product. Ginger can also be effective. More often, though, the cause of carsickness is psychological. Perhaps the dog associates riding in the car with unpleasantness (like going to the vet). Or perhaps he is frightened of the noise or motion of the car. Sometimes it's hard to figure exactly what came first, the sickness or the fear. Dogs who are anxious may express their anxiety through sickness, and those who get sick in the car may become increasingly anxious about it. Usually (not always), if the dog shows signs of anxiety (slavering, shaking) before even getting into the car, the problem is most likely anxiety-based.

To help your dog overcome fear of the car, take it slow and make the car a happy place. Try feeding him treats inside the car while the car is not running. Do this often enough for the dog to regard the car with approval. If your dog is afraid to even approach the car, you'll just have to give treats closer and closer to the car until he finally overcomes his fear. This may take some time.

After you've done this, repeat the routine with the car running. Go slow, as trying to hurry the desensitisation will backfire on you. When you actually start moving, go for very short trips to somewhere nice, even if it's only round the corner. Get out and walk the dog. Do this every day until the dog starts to really look forward to his daily car rides.

If your dog still retains his fear of the car, you may have to resort to a medical solution. Nonprescription products may help. In a few cases, you may need to get out the big guns and ask the vet for an anti-anxiety medication.

Travelling by Air

Everyone has horror stories about lost or injured pets on a flight, but you can reduce the risk of potential harm by following the law and using common sense. You will generally be required to supply a PETS certificate, which can be obtained from your veterinarian, and a valid rabies certificate before you'll be allowed to fly. Be forewarned: Many airlines will not transport a Bulldog, especially in the

summer months, because of breathing issues. This is why it's essential that you check out the airline's policy on pets before you go.

If you can get your Bulldog on a plane, try to book a nonstop, midweek flight. Try to fly during the evening or morning when it will be coolest.

Most airlines are also quite picky about the crate your Bulldog will be flying in. General rules are that the crate must:

- Be big enough to allow the dog to stand (without touching the top of the cage), turn around, and lie down;
- Have handles;
- Have a leak-proof flooring covered with absorbent material;
- Be clearly labelled with your name, home address, home telephone number, and destination contact information, as well as a designation of "Live Animal" with letters at least 1 inch high and arrows indicating the crate's upright position;
- Be ventilated on opposite sides, with exterior rims and knobs so that airflow is not impeded.

Get the crate well in advance so that your dog can get used to it before the big trip. And make sure your dog is flown as "baggage" (bad as that sounds) rather than as "freight" (which is worse). If he

Are You Allergic to Your Dog?

Before blaming your dog for your allergy, make sure it really is caused by the dog. Pets get blamed for a lot of allergies they are really not responsible for. Ask your doctor to test you for pet dander specifically before you blame your dog. If you do suffer allergies due to your pet, you're not alone. Fortunately, unless the allergy is severe, you can take steps to keep both your pet and your health.

First, create a special dog-free zone in your home. (The space should include your bedroom.) Just don't allow the dog in there at any time, and keep the door shut. Change your bed linen (including blankets and quilt) on a weekly basis. It's even better if you can use impermeable covers for the pillows and mattress. Even if the dog can't go in there, you'll carry allergen particles on your clothes, and pretty soon, they'll settle down into the mattress.

Buy some air purifiers and reduce to the bare minimum the number of carpets, curtains, and stuffed furniture in your house. Clean, vacuum, and dust frequently, and use a microfilter bag in the vacuum cleaner.

Bathe your dog frequently—at least once a week. It won't hurt him, and studies show that frequent bathing reduces allergens by over 75 percent.

Finally, consider immunotherapy. Allergy shots will reduce your symptoms, even if they can't eliminate them completely.

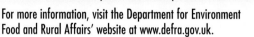

Pet Travel Scheme (PETS)

PETS is a system that permits companion animals from certain countries to travel to the UK without undergoing a period of quarantine. This scheme also applies to people in the UK who want to travel with their pets to other European Union countries.

For more information, visit the Department for Environment Food and Rural Affairs' website at www.defra.gov.uk.

goes as freight, he may be shipped on a different plane. Finally, keep your dog's nails short for the trip; you don't want them getting snagged in the carrier door.

Airline flight regulations with regard to pets change all the time. Contact the air carrier in advance for specific instructions.

Travelling by Bus or Train

In the UK dogs are generally allowed to use public transport, but must be kept on a lead. Check for any other restrictions before you travel.

If You Can't Take Your Dog

It is not always possible or even desirable to take your Bulldog along on every trip you take. In that case, you'll need to have a plan. If you're lucky, you can pop him over to a relative's house, but that's not an option for everyone.

Boarding Kennel

If you decide to use a commercial kennel, ask for a tour before you commit yourself—but commit early. Most kennels fill up a month in advance. Check on when you will be able to pick up your dog. Many do not have Sunday pickup. Good kennels:

- Are clean and free of excrement;
- Have both indoor and outdoor runs (preferably with solid partitions between them);
- Allow dogs frequent access to exercise and play;
- Provide appropriate grooming and bathing services;
- Require proof of vaccination, including bordetella;
- Have a vet clinic nearby for emergencies;
- Allow you to bring your dog's own food, bedding, and toys

if you desire;

- Are heated and *air-conditioned*, a must for the Bulldog in the summer;
- Love Bulldogs, appreciate their unique qualities, and understand their special needs.

Pet Sitter

Another option is a dog-sitting service. Some services will house-sit as well as pet-sit; others will make arrangements to come in and walk, feed, and play with your dog. If you are thinking of hiring a pet sitter, make sure to meet her first and note how she interacts with your Bulldog. Ask for references, experience, and check her ability to walk, or if necessary, medicate your dog. You may also want to test her knowledge by asking how she might handle certain dog problems, like vomiting or diarrhoea. If you like the candidate, make specific arrangements as to when she will be coming to care for your dog. Be sure that your pet sitter gets your contact information and that of your veterinarian.

Always make sure that your Bulldog is properly vaccinated before you travel with him.

4

FEEDING
Your Bulldog

You may have noticed that your Bulldog eats, well, almost anything! There's a reason for this. Although dogs are technically classed among the meat eaters, they are actually omnivorous creatures. They'll eat anything, from carrots to insects. They'll even eat rubbish if you let them. Bulldogs, especially, were not meant to be pampered pets, although that is what they have become. Most of them have an adventurous appetite and will eat whatever they can find. They didn't survive their earliest years by being coddled!

As you probably already know, what your dog eats has a tremendous impact on his well-being. However, to better understand what and how often to feed your Bulldog, it's important to understand how his digestive system works, as well as what nutrients are needed to keep him healthy.

UNDERSTANDING YOUR BULLDOG'S DIGESTIVE SYSTEM

Although we won't be discussing the entire digestive system of your Bulldog, we'll take a quick look down the old alimentary canal.

Nose

It's not a surprise to learn that dogs have much better sniffers than we do. (They don't always smell good, but they smell well.) How well they smell mostly depends on the size of the nose—the bigger the nose, the better the smeller. We humans have about 40 million odour receptors lining the olfactory epithelium membrane; big-nosed dogs may have about 200 million of them. Great nosers like Bloodhounds are good at their jobs because they have big noses in addition to a very determined attitude. I'm afraid your Bulldog will never match big-nosed breeds in this regard, but he's still better at it than we are.

Tongue

The tongue is a complicated, muscular organ that helps your dog take in, chew, and swallow food. Dogs also use it (rather inefficiently) to drink. In order to drink, a dog has to move his tongue around in the water bowl a lot, and he ends up taking in air as well as water, especially when he's a pup and still not very good at it. That's why a puppy will often end up with the hiccups after drinking. Dogs have taste buds on their tongues, too, just as we do, to distinguish flavours. The difference is that they don't have as many. They can also detect sour, sweet, and salt tastes. Their fewer taste buds make dogs more adventuresome in the matter of taste than humans. In other words, they tend to gobble down anything.

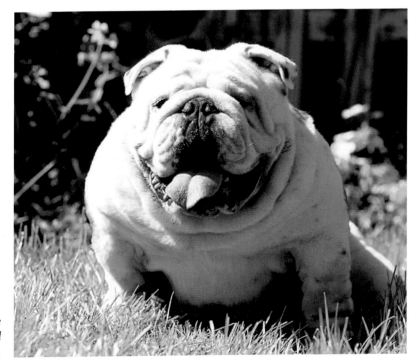

Most Bulldogs have adventurous appetites and will eat almost anything.

In the wild, where dogs lived in packs and competed for food, this was a valuable trait, but in today's world, this is a habit that can get dogs into trouble.

Salivary Glands

Dogs have four pairs of salivary glands that produce (what else?) saliva. Saliva is a remarkable substance that lubricates the inside of the mouth, helps food go down easier, and even contains enzymes that start the digestive process.

Jaw Bones

Like all dogs, cats, and humans, the jaws are made of two bones, the upper jaw, or "maxilla," and the lower jaw, or "mandible." The shape of the jaw determines how the teeth are placed. Bulldogs are known as brachycephalic, meaning they have short, wide muzzles.

Teeth

Both sets of jaws are lined with teeth. These include incisors for cutting and nibbling, canines for holding and tearing, premolars for cutting, shearing, and holding, and molars for grinding. Like most mammals, dogs have 28 deciduous, or baby, teeth that fall out and are replaced by 42 permanent teeth. The baby teeth start coming in when the puppy is three or four weeks old; the permanent teeth begin to erupt between the ages of three and four months. Most people can't wait for this to happen, because those little teeth are sharp. In some cases, the baby tooth doesn't fall out when it should. If this happens, misaligned permanent teeth can result. Ask your vet to remove the errant baby tooth.

The tooth has a crown above the gum and a root (or roots) below. The carnassial tooth, that big premolar, has three roots! In the centre of the tooth is the pulp, consisting of tissue, blood vessels, and nerves. Surrounding the pulp is the bone-hard dentin that makes up most of the tooth, and capping it all is the enamel, which is even harder than bone (and explains why dogs can eat bones). Around the whole tooth is periodontium, consisting of the alveolar bone, periodontal ligaments, cementum, and gingiva.

Oesophagus

Swallowing food takes the meal to its next destination, the oesophagus, which is a fairly wide, elastic tube lined with muscles.

The width of the oesophagus can be a problem; dogs are able to swallow much larger items than they can comfortably digest. Unfortunately, sharp bones and other bad things can go down the oesophagus with ease, only to become jammed in the stomach or small intestine.

Food is squeezed through the oesophagus by a process called peristalsis, in which the muscles contract in a wave beginning at the top and ending at the stomach. The oesophagus takes a sharp turn when it reaches the stomach to prevent food and stomach acids from being regurgitated back into the mouth.

Stomach: The Mixing Room

The dog's stomach is located within the left side of the abdomen. It contains glands that excrete mucus, hydrochloric acid, and digestive enzymes. The pylorus is a heavy band of muscle that closes the opening of the stomach leading into the intestine.

The stomach's job is to store and mix the food. Because of the dog's historic ability to find and gulp game at one shot, so to speak, the tummy is able to expand tremendously—holding between 2 and 20 pints (1.1 and 11 litres) of food, water, rubbish, or tinfoil, depending on the size, breed, and inclination of the dog.

The stomach is divided into three regions from front to back: the cardiac region, the fundic region, and the pyloric region. The glands of the fundic region add acids and a pepsin-producing enzyme that begin the digestion of protein in the food by breaking down connective and muscle tissue. Moreover, gastric acids help kill bacteria, parasites, and viruses that may have entered the gastrointestinal tract. Pepsin also plays a part in aiding the absorption of calcium, iron, and vitamin B_{12}.

The glands of the pyloric region produce a mucus that protects the stomach wall from the potentially destructive enzymes and acids of the fundic region. The mucus also helps to keep food moist.

Peristaltic waves spread though the stomach, which is sort of like a biological cement mixer. Food mixed with stomach slime is called "chyme." The food stays in the stomach for only three or four hours before moving along the digestive tract. When the chyme reaches the proper degree of sliminess, it slips through the pyloric sphincter to its next station, the small intestine.

Small Intestine: Where It All Gets Broken Down

The small intestine handles most of the tough work of digestion; it takes up almost a quarter of the total gastrointestinal volume of dogs.

The first part of the small intestine is the duodenum, which produces a thick alkaline excretion that neutralises the acid food from the tummy. The pancreas also ships in some digestive enzymes to help break down the food.

The intestinal lining is covered with small projections called villi. These projections, which are loaded with tiny microvilli, greatly increase the surface area of the small intestine. As a matter of fact, the villi of a medium-sized dog provide an absorptive surface the size of a good-sized bathroom. From the small intestines, nutrients pass into the bloodstream and lymph system. The small intestine also handles the transport of carbohydrates and proteins.

It takes about 36 hours for the digestive process to be complete, but moist food moves a lot faster than dry food.

Large Intestine: Solid Waste Removal

The dog's large intestine or colon has a large diameter, although it's shorter than the small intestine. In form, it's a simple tube that is shaped like a question mark. (There is a caecum, too, often described as part of the large intestine, but this appendix-like pouch is really off to the side at the juncture between the small and large intestines.)

The most important function of the large intestine is to dry out the waste material it receives from the small intestine, thereby conserving a great deal of water. Dogs would need to drink a lot more water if they didn't have a large intestine.

Rectum and Anus

Everything, of course, exits through the anus. The anal region comprises the anal canal and its associated structures. There are many glands associated with the anal region: the circum-anal glands, the anal glands proper, and the numerous microscopic glands located within the walls of the anal sacs. Sometimes these glands are called "scent" glands.

NUTRIENTS, VITAMINS, AND MINERALS

Now that you've seen how your dog's digestive system works, it's time to take a look at what goes into it—those all-important nutrients, vitamins, and minerals that make up your Bulldog's food.

Nutrients

Protein

About 50 percent of every cell in your dog's body is made of protein. Proteins are also critical for building enzymes, hormones, haemoglobin, and antibodies. All animals need protein for maintenance and healing, and young animals need it for growth. If a puppy doesn't get enough protein, his tissues and organs won't develop properly. Proteins are made up of important amino acids that animals need to grow and remain healthy. Dogs need more protein than people do; although no optimum level has been established, even 30 percent of the total calories in a dog's diet is not too much. Protein can be found in many foods, including meat, fish, eggs, and soybeans. However, all proteins are definitely not equal. Not all proteins are digestible proteins, and some are more digestible than others. Digestible proteins are those that can actually be absorbed through the gut wall into the body. This digestibility factor is what is really important, not the total amount of protein. For example, although they are actually omnivores, dogs cannot use proteins derived from plants very well; they need high-quality animal-based protein to do their best.

The proper balance of vitamins and minerals is essential to maintaining your Bulldog's health.

The digestibility factor of some cereals commonly found in dog food is only about 50 percent. Dogs function best on meat- or fish-derived protein; vegetable-derived protein can cause diarrhoea and is incomplete, meaning that it doesn't have enough of all of the different kinds of amino acids your dog needs. Ideally, a dog's diet should be about 75 percent meat, and the rest should be vegetables.

Unfortunately, although the dog food label lists the amount of protein in a food, it doesn't say where the protein comes from. Some kinds of protein are much more usable than others. Hair, for example, is almost entirely made of protein, but try living on a hair diet and see what happens to you!

If your dog doesn't get enough protein in his diet, he may show poor growth, a dull coat, and muscular wasting. (Only protein builds muscles.) Excess protein is usually excreted from the body, except in cases where the dog has kidney or liver damage.

Fat

Fats have twice the number of calories per gram as do protein or carbohydrates; they are packed with energy. Fats keep cells in good working order while adding texture to food and increasing its palatability. Dogs digest fats *very* efficiently and need a higher proportion of fat in their diets than we do to keep healthy. It's particularly important for dogs who have difficulty maintaining weight or who are picky eaters. (Fats contribute immensely to the palatability of foods, which is why cheesecake tastes better than parsnips.)

Dogs can use both plant and animal fats with equal ease. However, oils derived from plants provide large amounts of essential fatty acids (EFAs). These acids are needed for many biological functions. In the wild, dogs eat portions of the vegetable matter contained in their prey's stomach. This presumably supplies them with some EFAs.

Most commercial dry dog foods contain between 5 and 10 percent fat, sufficient for sedentary dogs. Fat also makes food taste better, which is why most dogs prefer any tinned meat to dry food (kibble). Fats also deliver the fat-soluble vitamins A, D, E, and K and help make a healthy coat. Too much fat, however, especially when given all at once, results in pancreatic problems. And of course, it makes dogs gain weight. Insufficient fat makes for a dry coat and poor growth.

Dogs who do lots of work for long periods in the cold, like Huskies running a race, need more fat than the average Bulldog. Good commercial foods are properly supplied with the right amount of fat to fulfil a dog's needs throughout his various life stages.

Carbohydrates

Sugar, starches, and dietary fibre are all carbohydrates. They provide very efficient energy and serve as building blocks for other

Protein Power

Signs that your Bulldog is not getting enough protein:

- Poor growth
- Dull coat
- Muscular wasting

biological components. They are also a heat source for the body when they are metabolised for energy. They can be stored as glycogen or converted to fat. They also help regulate protein and fat metabolism.

Dietary fibres help move food through the intestinal tract and provide bulk, helping an animal feel full without extra calories.

Scientists are still trying to figure out the precise place of carbohydrates in a dog's diet. Dogs can use them to make energy, but are they actually needed? Test results suggest that they may be, at least for pregnant and nursing dogs. It's not a major issue, since nearly every dog food and dog biscuit in the country is loaded with carbohydrates. Excess carbohydrates are stored as fat and can lead to obesity.

Equally important as what nutrients your dog needs is the proportion in which he gets them. This is partly dependent on his individual needs, health, and life stage. Growing puppies, healthy adults, and elderly dogs need different amounts of protein and nutrients.

Vitamins

According to *Stedman's Medical Dictionary*, a vitamin is "one of a group of organic substances, present in minute amounts in natural foodstuffs, which are essential to normal metabolism." Vitamins are naturally present only in tiny amounts, but they are essential for life.

Dogs and people both need vitamins for thousands of chemical reactions that take place in the body. Along with minerals and enzymes, vitamins help with digestion, reproduction, blood clotting, and the normal development of muscle, bone, skin, and hair. Vitamins are also important in the way the body uses protein, carbohydrates, and fats.

Vitamins come in two major varieties, fat soluble and water soluble. Fat-soluble vitamins can be stored by the body, but water-soluble vitamins are excreted quickly and should be supplied every day in the diet.

Because vitamins are present in very small quantities in most foods, many people decide to supplement. This can't hurt with water-soluble vitamins, which are only found within the body in tiny amounts. Fat-soluble vitamins, on the other hand, are usually stored in special fat storage cells called lipocytes. They can build up within the body and may cause trouble if oversupplemented. People worry about toxicities associated with large amounts of fat-soluble vitamins, especially A and D. This won't happen with a regular diet, but it is possible to overdose your dog with them if you supplement carelessly. Always consult your veterinarian before supplementing these vitamins.

Vitamin A (fat soluble)

Vitamin A and beta-carotene seem to enhance immune functions and may help to prevent some kinds of cancer. Be careful not to oversupplement, however. Large amounts of vitamin A are poisonous. A couple of carrots a day will do perfectly.

Vitamin D (fat soluble)

Vitamin D is really a group of compounds that help regulate calcium and phosphorus in the body. It's not known whether dogs need vitamin D added to their diet, since their skin can activate it from the sun's ultraviolet rays. Vitamin D can be found in fish oils, egg yolks, and many meat and milk products. However, if your Bulldog spends much time outside, he probably gets lots of it anyway. Insufficient amounts of vitamin D can cause rickets and other bone problems. Too much can cause hardening of soft tissues, diarrhoea, and weight loss.

Vitamin E (tocopherols) (fat soluble)

Vitamin E is a potent antioxidant that helps prevent the oxidation of the unsaturated fatty acids found in cell membranes. Vitamin E helps produce prostaglandins, which regulate blood pressure, muscle contraction, and reproductive functions. In fact, vitamin E may be a good supplement for neutered pets. One form is used in the pet food industry as a preservative. As a preservative in pet food, vitamin E operates much as it does in tissues, preventing the oxidation of the fats that makes the food "go bad."

Vitamin E is found in polyunsaturated vegetable oils like wheat germ oil, corn oil, and sunflower oil. The best vegetable source is probably safflower oil, which contains the very active alpha tocopherol form of vitamin E. Whole grain cereals, cod liver oil, and egg yolk also contain vitamin E. Deficiencies in vitamin E can weaken the immune system. There seem to be no known toxicities with too much.

Vitamin K (quinones) (fat soluble)

Vitamin K was the last vitamin to be discovered. Dogs generally don't need vitamin K added to their diet; they can make enough of the vitamin from the bacterial synthesis in their intestines. However, when the animal is on a course of antibiotics (which can destroy one form of vitamin K), it is sometimes wise to supplement

Did You Know?

Many people are uncertain whether their dogs are getting enough vitamins and minerals in their diets. While this is a legitimate concern, it's easy to go overboard the other way. Puppies are particularly vulnerable to the dangers of oversupplementation. Don't add minerals or vitamins to your puppy's diet without a recommendation from your veterinarian.

by feeding vegetables like spinach or kale, which produce vitamin K. Antibiotics kill off some of the normal intestinal bacteria necessary for vitamin K_2 synthesis. Vitamin K helps blood clot as well.

Vitamin C (water soluble)

One of the most interesting of the vitamins is vitamin C. Vitamin C comes in two forms: dehydroascorbic acid and ascorbic acid. Ascorbic acid mixes easily with water and is readily absorbed through the intestinal wall. It also enters the urine. Very little is stored within the body. Dogs can manufacture their own ascorbic acid from glucose, although humans cannot.

While some people think vitamin C cures hip dysplasia, it does not. Hip dysplasia is a genetic abnormality, and not even vitamin C can change genetic structure. Some studies seem to indicate that large doses of vitamin C do result in lessened joint pain, although it can't treat the underlying condition itself.

It's probably helpful to supplement your dog's diet with vitamin C, especially in fast-growing puppies, pregnant bitches, lactating mother dogs, and working dogs. This is a safe, nontoxic vitamin. However, there is controversy raging over the function of vitamin C in the canine diet. Unlike human beings, dogs can manufacture vitamin C themselves, so conventional wisdom tells us that dogs don't need it added to their food. Some nutritionists claim it can actually be dangerous to the kidneys. Other experts, however, tout the value of vitamin C. For one thing, although dogs can make their own vitamin C, they seem less efficient at doing so than all of the other mammals who can manufacture their own. However, dogs who receive large supplements of vitamin C may lose the ability to produce it for themselves. Because vitamin C has antihistamine properties, some theorists believe it helps protect against certain canine allergies. Others think it plays a role in fighting arthritis, along with vitamin E and the mineral selenium. Vitamin C may even fight cancer, both by preventing the occurrence of the disease and as a dietary supplement for cancer patients.

Don't supplement your Bulldog's diet without speaking to your vet.

Thiamin (water soluble)

Thiamin, or vitamin B_1, converts glucose to energy and is needed for the normal function of muscles and nerves. A deficiency of thiamin results in loss of appetite, weakness, loss of reflexes, loss of nerve control, and death. It's pretty rare to have a thiamin deficiency; it usually occurs in animals who have been fed only raw fish, especially catfish, smelt, or herring, all of which contain an enzyme called thiaminase that destroys thiamin. If your dog is living only on raw fish, stop right now.

Riboflavin (water soluble)

Riboflavin (vitamin B_2) is important for growth, muscle development, and maintaining a healthy coat. It is found in organ meats and dairy products. A deficiency of riboflavin causes poor growth, eye abnormalities, rear leg weakness, and heart failure. Such animals may also have fainting episodes, termed "collapsing syndrome."

Pyridoxine (water soluble)

Pyridoxine (vitamin B_6) helps the body use amino acids. It is found in many foods but is destroyed by processing. Pyridoxine deficiency results in anaemia, poor growth, kidney stones, tooth cavities, skin lesions, and even death. Pyridoxine is found in meats (especially organ meat), whole grains, and vegetables.

Biotin (water soluble)

Biotin helps maintain healthy skin and hair and is important for growth, digestion, and muscle function. Your Bulldog produces about half the biotin he needs from his own intestines; the rest comes from meat, milk, eggs, and legumes.

Minerals

A dietary mineral is any inorganic component of a food. Like vitamins, minerals are substances necessary for an animal's health. Dietary minerals are generally classed into two main groups: macrominerals (sulphur, calcium, phosphorus, magnesium, and the electrolytes sodium, potassium, and chloride) which are consumed in gram quantities per day, and trace minerals like iron, zinc, copper, iodine, and selenium, needed in milligrams or micrograms per day. A third class includes the ultratrace minerals that have been shown to be necessary in laboratory animals but not in dogs.

Minerals participate in nearly every function of the body. They build teeth and bone, serve as parts of enzymes, and are a vital component of the blood and other body fluids. Minerals also play a role in muscle contraction, nerve impulse transmission, and cell membrane permeability.

Calcium (Ca)

Calcium, composing about 2 percent of body weight, is the most abundant mineral in your dog's body. Calcium is the major inorganic component of bone. In fact, about 99 percent of the body's calcium is found in the skeleton. Calcium is plentiful in dairy products and legumes. Foods high in calcium include bones, eggshell, and leafy green vegetables. In dog food, high levels of calcium are found in poultry by-product meal, lamb meal, and fish meal. This is mostly because of their bone content. Meat without bone is a very poor source of calcium. And milk, while high in calcium, has very little magnesium, which is necessary to metabolise the calcium.

Calcium forms and strengthens bones and teeth, helps in blood clotting, and aids metabolism. A calcium deficiency results in slower, incomplete growth and poor bone and muscle. However, too much calcium, especially when not balanced with phosphorus, can lead to skeletal deformities and joint breakdown.

Phosphorus (P)

After calcium, phosphorus is the most plentiful component of bones and teeth. Phosphorus

Minerals

Minerals are essential for nearly every function of the body. They:

- Build teeth and bones
- Serve as parts of enzymes
- Are a vital component of the blood
- Play a role in muscle contraction

Dietary minerals play an important role in building teeth and bone.

is also involved in most of the chemical reactions in the body. It aids growth and is necessary for muscle contraction. Protein-rich foods also contain phosphorus in abundance. Meat, legumes, oilseeds, and dairy products are rich sources. When phosphorus is incorrectly balanced with calcium, dogs can develop loose teeth and constipation.

Magnesium (Mg)

Magnesium is interdependent with calcium and phosphorus for bone development. Just as calcium stimulates muscles, magnesium helps them relax. Magnesium is found in bones and bone meal, oilseed and protein supplements, legumes, dairy products, and unrefined grain and fibre. Dogs whose diet is low in magnesium could suffer from poor appetite and irritability, as well as muscle weakness.

Manganese (Mn)

Manganese is a component of many cell enzymes, particularly those involved with the production of energy. Sources include cereals and menhaden fish oil. Deficiency is rare. Manganese is a relatively nontoxic mineral, even in large amounts.

Copper (Cu)

Copper is a component of many enzymes that catalyse reactions involving oxygen. Copper is linked to zinc, and its metabolism is

Like calcium, phosphorus is an integral component of healthy bones and teeth.

related to that of iron. In fact, copper is necessary for the absorption and transport of iron. It is essential for all cells and enables the incorporation of iron into haemoglobin. It is found in meat, especially organ meat, and bones. A deficiency is rare, found most often in diets lacking sufficient meat intake.

Sodium (Na) and Chloride or Chlorine (Cl)

Sodium and chloride are called electrolytes. Both sodium and chloride help to regulate the acid-base balance and maintain the balance of dissolved substances inside and outside the cells (called the osmotic pressure). Sodium is needed for the absorption of sugars and amino acids in the small intestine. Sodium, together with potassium, is necessary for the transmission of nerve impulses. Chloride forms hydrochloric acid in the stomach.

Sodium and chloride are found in salt and cereals, fish, eggs, dried whey, and poultry by-product meal. A deficiency (very rare) causes excess urination, salt hunger, pica, and weight loss. Obese dogs, hypertensive dogs, and dogs with kidney disease or certain endocrine conditions should probably lay off the salt. Most commercial foods are loaded with the stuff.

Iron (Fe)

Iron is present in every cell of the body, but its greatest concentration is in the proteins haemoglobin and myoglobin. Haemoglobin is found in the red blood cells and transports oxygen from the lungs to the tissues. The best source of iron for dogs is from meat, especially organ meat like liver, spleen, and lungs. It is rare to see a dog with an iron deficiency unless he has been on a vegetarian diet. Except in extreme cases, do not supplement iron. If you're giving your dog a vitamin/mineral supplement, choose one without iron. Since meat and dairy products abound in iron, normal dogs don't need an iron supplement. Iron can be toxic in large concentrations.

Selenium (Se)

Dogs need less selenium than any other commonly recognised trace mineral. It is also toxic in very small amounts. However, selenium helps protect cell membranes from oxidative damage, much like vitamin E. Vitamin E can replace the requirement for selenium in the body, but selenium cannot substitute for vitamin E. Selenium does not cross the blood brain barrier like vitamin E. Selenium is found in eggs, liver, and cereals. However, selenium in fish is not very bioavailable.

Iodine (I)

Iodine makes up part of the thyroid hormones thyroxine (T4) and triiodothyronine (T3), which regulate the metabolic rates of the body. The iodine your dog consumes ends up mostly in his thyroid gland. Iodine is found in milk, fish, eggs, poultry, and iodised salt. Iodine deficiency is rare, found mostly in dogs who receive a diet composed solely of meat.

Zinc

Zinc is an essential mineral that is added to today's commercial diets. However, some puppies, pregnant bitches, performance dogs, or pets with skin problems may require a supplement. It also improves the hair coat. This is because zinc is not well absorbed by the body. Further, plants and fibres contain substances that bind zinc, so dogs fed a mostly vegetable-based diet may develop a zinc deficiency. Too much calcium in the diet can also bind zinc. Dogs with inflammatory bowel disease may develop zinc deficiency. You can find a zinc supplement in good vitamin supplements and in many fatty acid supplements. Zinc is especially important, as it is needed for normal metabolism. A diet deficient in zinc will result in thin hair and crusty dermatitis.

Now that you have a basic understanding of what nutrients, vitamins, and minerals your dog needs to remain healthy, it's crucial that you learn how to interpret dog food labels to determine what foods are best for your Bulldog.

Read the label before you feed your Bulldog any commercial food.

DOG FOOD LABELS

While understanding a dog food label is not more difficult than classical Greek, it is not much easier, either. Still, the careful consumer can figure out at least some of it.

Of course, every pet food manufacturer can tell you why that particular brand of food is best for dogs, and often why another type of food isn't so good. Dry food, tinned food, natural food, raw diets, even prescription foods for certain conditions all have a place and can all be appropriate, depending on the dog and the owner. So, whats a well-meaning Bulldog owner to do? Should you just close your eyes and pick one?

In the UK, pet food is controlled by the Food Standards Agency (FSA), which has to adhere to EC guidelines. Manufacturers also belong to the Pet Food Manufacturer's Association (PFMA), which, in turn, follows guidelines laid down by the European Pet Food Industry Federation (FEDIAF). Every label contains the following information:

- Ingredients list
- Additives (preservatives, colourings, etc.)
- Vitamins
- Best before date
- Bar code
- Batch number
- Net weight
- Name and address.

The nutritional standards stated in law and given on pet food labels are only minimum requirements. Do you want your Bulldog to subsist, or do you want your Bulldog's food to go above and beyond the minimum requirement for avoiding malnutrition?

Many premium foods include ingredients that may add valuable phytochemicals (nonnutritive plant substances that may have important disease-fighting effects). Many are customised for very specific situations, like dogs with arthritis or for large breeds. You need to find out what is the best choice for your Bulldog.

That means you must also know your Bulldog and the nutrients he needs for his life stage. Is he a growing puppy? Maybe a puppy food isn't the best choice because Bulldogs need to grow slowly for proper bone density. Or, maybe a puppy food custom formulated for slow bone growth in puppies is the best choice. Does your Bulldog have sensitive skin? He may need a unique protein source like a fish-based food, with its omega-3 fatty acids and non-allergenic salmon.

You aren't alone in making a decision about the best food for your dog. Talk to your vet or breeder about your concerns if you want help in choosing the food that will help your Bulldog grow strong bones, supple skin, and shiny soft coat. Food can help to keep your Bulldog in a state of glowing health through his adult years, and best meet his needs as a veteran.

But first, let's consider the different kinds of dog foods available to you.

TYPES OF FOOD

Your choice of what to feed your dog is practically unlimited: dry food, tinned food, semi-moist, "people food," or any mixture thereof. I am not going to tell you that only one kind is right for you and your dog. Many factors come into play: convenience, expense, nutritional value, taste, availability, allergies, and other things. What's right for one dog is not right for all. One rule I do apply is, "Don't feed your Bulldog something he dislikes." Yes, he will eat almost anything if he gets hungry enough, rather than starve. So would I, but that doesn't mean I'd like it. Mealtimes

The Calcium/Phosphorus Ratio

Ideally, the calcium/phosphorus ratio should range between 1:1 and 2:1, with 1.1:1 or 1.2:1 being ideal. A diet that is loaded with meats high in phosphorus and low in calcium, or a plant-based diet high in phytates with a calcium content greater than 2.5 percent (DM), can lead to trouble. However, if your dog is receiving the correct amounts of calcium and phosphorus, the ratio takes care of itself. The ratio is more important for puppies, especially large-breed puppies, than for adult dogs.

should be pleasurable for everyone, so why not shop around until you find something nutritious that your dog really enjoys? If he seems to like something for a while, then gets bored with it, change his food. It's not difficult.

Whatever you choose, go for quality. The difference between the best and worst is just a few pounds a bag, but the difference in nutrition can add healthy years to your dog's life.

Commercial Foods

An American living in England essentially invented commercial dog food by baking up biscuits of wheat meal, meat, and vegetables. In the early twentieth century customers could find some bulk dry dog foods made from meal and pellets, but they barely resembled the dry dog food in stores today. Around this time tinned dog food also debuted made from horsemeat.

You can avoid the worst food by sticking to some simple guidelines.

1. Avoid dog foods containing "by-products." Meat by-products are those parts of the animal not deemed fit for human consumption. While some by-products are both healthy and tasty to dogs, many more are not. Avoid them.

2. Avoid food laden with grain or cereal by-products. These ingredients are the part of the plant left over after the milling process. They are technically called "fragments," but they appear in many guises on the label. The carbohydrates in food should be whole grains. Many dogs are allergic to soy, so stay away from it.

3. Good food should not contain sweeteners, artificial flavours, colours, or preservatives. The best dog foods are preserved naturally with vitamin E (tocopherols) or vitamin C (ascorbic acid).

4. Select food with the specific name of a meat (beef, chicken, turkey) as the first ingredient. Avoid foods whose label lists a generic "meat" or "poultry." Unfortunately, just because a product has "beef" as the first ingredient doesn't mean that the product is mostly beef. Some companies engage in a nefarious practice called "splitting." If they can possibly do so, they will divide the cereal products up into separate categories, like "rice" and then "brown rice." Added together, there may be more rice than beef. But because the companies are allowed to list them as separate ingredients, beef is listed first.

Did You Know?

Avoid feeding your Bulldog high-fat dairy products, processed meat, sweets, and chocolate. Chocolate is toxic to dogs, while high-fat foods can lead to pancreatitis and obesity. Very salty products, like processed meats and sugary foods like sweets are not natural to a dog's diet (or even to ours).

Dry Food (Kibble)

This is the most common type of dog food, but the premium and super-premium brands of dry food available today are far superior to the dry food available a decade ago.

The manufacturing process is largely the same. While a few speciality foods are baked rather than extruded, extrusion is generally the most efficient and cost-effective manufacturing process for dry food. Ingredients like meat and grains are combined, cooked, then forced under high presure through an extruder to form noodle-like shapes that can then be sliced or formed into dry food of various sizes. The food is then dried, coated with supplemental ingredients like vitamins, minerals, preserving oils, and nutraceuticals (like probiotics to aid in digestion and glucosamine to support healthy joints), then packaged in a bag and shipped off to pet shops and supermarkets.

The difference between dry food in the twenty-first century and the dry food of just a few decades ago has to do with the ingredients that go into the mix. Veterinary nutritional science has discovered a lot about what dogs need, not just to maintain an illness-free baseline, but to thrive at their healthy best. While you can still buy inexpensive dry food with low-quality ingredients, this is akin to feeding your children a diet of junk food. Sure, they might survive on it, but they will probably begin to suffer health problems. Many Bulldogs fed a poor diet gain too much weight, have loose, smelly stools and suffer from itchy skin, a dull coat and low energy.

Many Bulldogs prefer larger kibble, and some research has suggested that dry food, like kibble, helps reduce tartar buildup on teeth.

Fortunately, premium foods have changed all that, and if you choose to feed your Bulldog dry food, you will probably find that the cost of premium food is well worth it. Using high quality ingredients designed for maximum health, these foods result in better health, and because they are more nutritionally dense, dogs don't need to eat as much of them. You'll also find it is much more pleasant picking up after Bulldogs - in the garden or on walks - if they are eating a premium diet.

Premium dry food typically contains meat and/or meat meal (meat meal is meat with all the moisture removed) as the first

Did You Know?

Food should be served at room temperature if possible, not directly from the refrigerator or a hot oven. Very cold food eaten rapidly can make a dog vomit, not to mention experience that ice cream headache feeling. On the other hand, some food seems more palatable to dogs if slightly warmed.

ingredient. Common choices include chicken, beef and lamb, but you can also find formulas made with fish and venison. Because ingredients on the label are listed in order according to how much the food contains, a food listing meat first means the food has more meat than any other ingredient. Because most dogs need high quality meat protein in their diets, foods listing meat first are good choices for Bulldogs.

Premium dry food also typically contains grains like rice, oats, barley, wheat, soyabeans (not really a grain but often used in pet foods) and maize. Some dogs have trouble digesting maize, soya and/or wheat, or may have allergic reactions to these grains. Premium dry food may also contain organ meats, eggs and dairy products, animal and/or vegetable fat, fresh or dried vegetables (like carrots and kale), fresh or dried fruits (like apples). They might also contain various other ingredients like nuts, seeds (including the omega-3 rich flaxseed), vegetable and nut oils and supplemental ingredients such as vitamins, minerals, preservatives (often vitamin E oil), probiotics (like the friendly bacteria in yogurt and nutraceuticals like glucosamine for joint health. Look for food that contains ingredients whose names you recognise or with explanations of ingredients you don't recognise.

Dry food comes in bags and stays fresh for about a month, but can turn stale if exposed to air and dogs (not to mention any stray creatures in the house from ants to mice) could easily tear through the paper bag for a nibble. Keep dry food in a plastic container with a tight-fitting lid and only buy as much as your Bulldog will eat in two to three weeks. Few food choices can beat dry food for convenience and most Bulldogs will happily devour their dry food. Some people like to feed their dogs a basic diet of kibble, with different added foods every day, like green beans, carrots, gravy, or tinned meat. This plan gives your dog adequate nutrition and variety.

Tinned Food

Tinned dog food looks a lot more like meat than a scoop of dry food and dogs often love the taste. Tinned food is mixed, cooked and tinned without the moisture being removed, so the percentages on the tin label look a lot different than the percentages on the bag of dry food. The percentage of protein in a dry food, for example, looks much higher than in a tinned food, because the tinned food has so much water. If a food is 90 percent water, then the remaining 10 percent of the food contains the part that has the nutrition, so this skews the percentages. To accurately compare, you have to make a few calculations, but in general, tinned food generally has a higher protein.

Dry food is nutritionally denser than tinned food, so your dog will need to eat more to get the nutrition he needs. Many dogs enjoy a big spoonful of tinned food mixed into their dry food, however. Like dry food, tinned dog food comes in a wide variety of economical, premium and super premium brands. Also, like dry food, the premium and super-premium varieties typically use higher quality ingredients and are probably worth the higher price.

Semi-Moist Food

Semi-moist food is about 25 percent water and can be just as high in sugar, in the form of corn syrup, beet pulp, sucrose, and caramel. Your dog does not need this stuff, which promotes obesity and tooth decay. The shelf life of these products is also lower than either tinned or dry food.

People Food

Considering what the commercial pet food market is like, it's all right to feed your dog most food that is healthy for human beings. The old warnings about not feeding your dog table scraps were a

Storing Food

Food stored improperly can become loaded with moulds and other deadly toxins. To reduce the chances of your dog becoming a victim, be sure to use the freshest foods available. If you use a commercial food, check the manufacturing date. Do not buy in bulk; it may save you some money, but it's dangerous for your dog. Smaller bags get used more quickly and stay fresher longer.

Store the food in a dry, cool place away from sunlight. It's best if you keep the food in the house or some other place with a stable temperature. Temperature fluctuations can produce moisture in the food storage container that may lead to the development of mould or toxins. Most food should be kept in its original packaging or in a special airtight container. Don't use a plastic rubbish bin, even a clean one. These containers are often made of plastics that produce offensive or dangerous vapours.

If the food smells bad or if your dog suddenly refuses to eat it (while otherwise retaining his appetite), throw the stuff out, or take it back to the point of purchase for a refund.

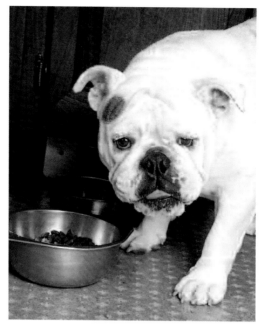

Commercial foods provide a convenient way for you to feed your Bulldog.

masterpiece of propaganda served up with relish by dog food manufacturers. Dogs thrive on fresh vegetables, chicken, beef, and fish. Many dogs also like fruit, including apple slices, melon, banana, and berries. (I once had a dog who carefully picked blackberries from our bushes.) Low-fat plain yogurt and small amounts of cottage cheese are also delightful treats. Large amounts of dairy foods can be troublesome, however; most dogs don't have the necessary enzymes to process them.

Avoid cramming your dog with junk food you shouldn't be eating yourself, such as biscuits, crisps, chocolate (which is potentially toxic to dogs), hot dogs, and pickles. Many of these foods cause gastrointestinal upset, which can result in vomiting and diarrhoea. This is especially likely with high-fat foods, to which your dog is probably not accustomed. The pancreas can really take a hit from these items, and your dog could get pancreatitis.

BARF Diet (Bones and Raw Food) / Frozen Raw Diet

Raw diets consist of raw meat, uncooked bones, ground vegetables and fruits, and sometimes cooked whole grains like rice or oatmeal. Some people, including many holistic vets, strongly believe that dogs will be much healthier on a diet closer to what they once ate in the wild. When dogs had to fend for themselves, they would typically eat small animals, including their meat, organs, bones and stomach contents (which typically included digested plant food). A bowl of dry food doesn't look much like a rabbit or a chicken.

A raw meat diet must be carefully formulated to include all the necessary nutrients. A meat only diet will quickly result in serious nutritional deficiencies! But proponents of the raw diet say that raw meat and raw bone are the foods nature intended for dogs to eat, that their digestive tracts are designed to handle the bacteria in raw meat, and that dogs on this diet thrive and are generally the picture of health. The bones keep dogs' teeth healthy and provide necessary minerals. The vegetables and grains provide necessary fibre.

But raw meat diets are controversial. Some vets believe the potential for food-borne illness is too great and that raw meat in the state it is available today, just isn't good for dogs. They also worry about the dangers of ingesting bone fragments, if raw bones are included (never feed a dog any cooked bone, as these splinter easily and could cause internal damage).

Other vets believe commercially prepared pet food is far more dangerous, and the root of many chronic diseases in dogs today, such as allergies, cancer, even chronic behavioural problems. This is a sensitive subject and you can get ten different opinions from ten different veterinary surgeons.

The problem with raw diets, even for those who think they are the ideal diet for dogs, is that some people may find them unpleasant to prepare. Plus, the constant contact with raw meat can be a health hazard for humans, especially children. Enter the commercially prepared frozen raw diet! These convenient products eliminate the mess and guesswork from feeding a raw diet. Pet shops specialising in holistic/natural products often stock raw diets, which are kept in the freezer. Just defrost and serve.

Variety: The Spice of Life

The best single thing you can do to ensure that your dog is getting the nutrients he needs is to feed him a variety of different foods. This will not only make eating more pleasurable for him, but if you start early enough, it will help protect him from developing allergies. I also strongly urge you to supply your dog with something other than a steady diet of commercial foods. Well-chosen, lower-fat table scraps will not only reduce his risk of bloat (this is proven), but they can boost the quality of every meal by providing nutrients of the highest calibre (not by-products).

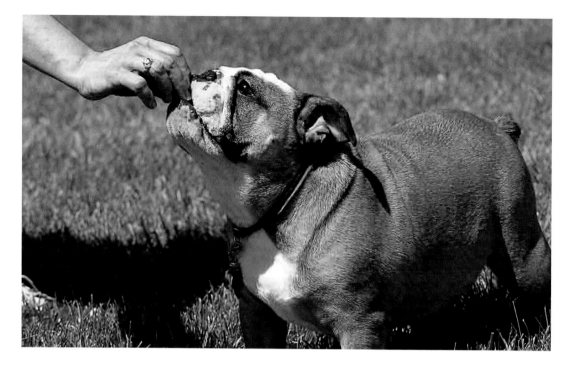

Treats fed in tiny quantities are an effective way to reward your Bulldog.

It is well worthwhile having a chat with your own vet next time you visit the surgery, or maybe someone at your training club has experience of feeding a raw diet to their dogs.

Homecooked Meals

For people who want to provide a homemade diet for their dogs but aren't comfortable with the whole raw concept, the homemade cooked diet may be just the ticket. Many people cook for their dogs, usually combining meat (such as chicken, turkey, beef, lamb or fish) and chopped vegetables with rice, oatmeal or barley. This might sound like a complicated nutritional balancing act, but if a dog's diet consists of a wide variety of healthy meats, cooked grains and chopped vegetables, plus other healthy additions like plain yogurt, cottage cheese, eggs and chopped fruits, the nutrition will take care of itself. Be sure to avoid unhealthy and unsafe foods such as onions, chocolate, excessive sugar and processed food; include some raw crunchy vegetables for good dental health, such as baby carrots and broccoli florets. It's simple common sense, but you still may want to consult professional resources before cooking for your dog, to be sure you add all the right supplements.

Talk to your breeder or vet if you are considering a homemade cooked diet, to be sure you are giving your dog everything he needs.

Treats

Most people enjoy giving their dog treats, and it's a harmless enough activity, as long as you don't overfeed. However, some treats are definitely poor choices for your dog.

The popular use of cow hooves as dog treats is dangerous. Cow hooves are the number-one cause of broken teeth in dogs. Although wild dogs chew the hooves of recent kills, fresh hooves are much more pliable than the smoked variety commonly available in shops today.

Most Bulldogs like rawhide chews, sometimes too much. They chew them up like gum and then swallow them. The rawhide can stick in a Bulldog's throat. Even if he gets it down, it's not doing his digestive system any good. Some rawhide treats are basted with flavours that disagree with the canine digestive system, causing diarrhoea. If you notice this, switch to plain rawhide treats, or omit them altogether. Dogs also have strong opinions when it comes to the perfect flavour in treats, but despite the recent plethora of melon, vanilla, and peanut butter delights, most dogs like liver. There's no accounting for taste.

If your dog is overweight, replace high-calorie treats with nutritious, crispy carrots, and add fresh vegetables like broccoli to your dog's dinner. Just as with humans, the key is a low-fat, high-fibre diet. Unless you're an expert on home-prepared foods, use a high-quality weight-loss commercial brand. The manufacturer has done the hard part by providing the correct amounts of vitamins and minerals.

Treats are not only a pleasant dietary interlude for your dog, but they are also (in tiny quantities) great for rewards during training. Bulldogs like praise, but like most other breeds, they do respond best to food.

Bones

Bones are naturally balanced sources of calcium and phosphorous, and dogs adore them. However, cooked bones are dangerous, because they can easily splinter and damage your dog's

Grass Anyone?

If you catch your dog eating grass, he's not abnormal. Most dogs attempt to eat grass from time to time, although they can't digest it. No one knows why they do it. Some suggest dogs who eat grass have upset tummies and do so to make themselves throw up. Others suggest they just like the taste of the stuff.

impact of arthritis. Over twenty-five percent of all adult dogs in the United Kingdom are overweight, a fact that affects their health, enjoyment of life, and ability to participate in normal dog activities. Bulldogs are particularly prone to obesity. No matter how much fun it is to feed your dog, and no matter how much he enjoys eating, remember: Obesity will shorten his life.

Obesity is defined as being 10 to 25 percent above the ideal weight for your dog. Look at your Bulldog from above: He should resemble an hourglass. Too much bulge in the waist indicates that your dog needs to be put on a diet. If you run your thumbs along your dog's spine, you should be able to feel each rib. If you must put pressure on the rib cage to feel the ribs, he's overweight. (If you can actually see your dog's ribs, he's too thin.) When viewed from the side, you should see a "tucked-up" waist.

Although most cases of obesity are due to the fatal combination of overfeeding and underexercising, in a few instances a medical condition like hypothyroidism or insulin imbalance could be at fault. Don't put your dog on a weight-loss programme until you check with your veterinarian to make sure there are no underlying medical problems.

The best way to control your dog's weight is to provide him with the proper amount of food for his ideal size. Your vet can help you to determine that. I know you enjoy feeding your dog treats, but they add weight. If you do like to treat your dog, cut down on

How Much Is Too Much?

Research at the Ralston Purina Pet Care Centre indicates that an inactive 50-pound adult dog requires 1,450 calories a day in the summer. (That's your Bulldog, all right!) The same dog requires 1,800 calories during moderate work or training and 2,160 calories when performing heavy work. Don't worry about these latter figures—your Bulldog won't be doing any heavy work. It's important to remember that these calorie requirements are for dogs in general, not for Bulldogs in particular, let alone yours. Age, temperature, and activity level are important qualifications. It's just not possible to precisely determine how many calories a particular dog will actually require. Luckily, you don't need to know exactly how many calories your dog actually needs. Just keep an eye on him. If he starts looking pudgy, reduce his intake, and if he starts looking too thin, increase his intake.

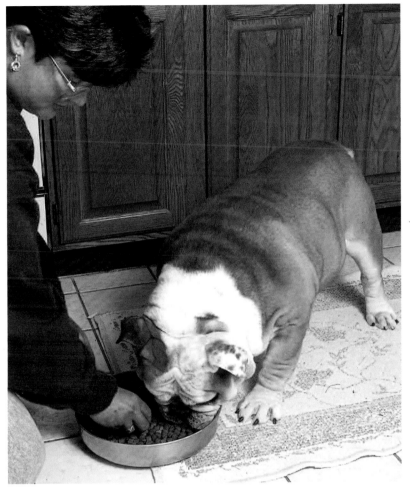

An adult Bulldog should only be fed twice a day to prevent him from becoming overweight.

the meals proportionately, or give low-calorie treats like carrot slivers.

In some cases, you may want to resort to a commercial low-calorie food. Pick one that includes specific weight-loss directions. If you feed a dog according to the regular feeding directions, he won't lose weight. Regular feeding directions are designed to maintain a dog's weight.

Another way to keep your dog's weight in check is to provide him with plenty of healthy exercise. Dogs like this option much better than cutting down on their chow, too. If you are starting an exercise weight-loss programme for your dog, check with your vet before embarking on anything strenuous.

C h a p t e r

GROOMING
Your Bulldog

lthough grooming your dog well will certainly make him feel like a Crufts champion, it does more than improve his looks. It is also a great way to keep him in good health and cement your bond with him. Pretty impressive for a few minutes of brushing a couple of times a week!

Grooming your dog puts him in the centre of attention, where all Bulldogs long to be. You not only get to make him over, but you also get to check him out for bumps, growths, sores, and bruises. It's a first-line defence against disease. In addition, by removing dead and dirty hair and stimulating the skin, grooming also aids your Bulldog in avoiding skin infections and irritations. Spreading natural oils throughout the skin helps the coat retain its lustre. In addition, well-groomed dogs look and smell better and are consequently more likely to be included in family activities.

BRUSHING

Most Bulldogs love to be gently brushed, so do it about three times a week, using a soft bristle or rubber brush. You can get away with once a week or even every other week, but more frequent brushing is best. The general practice is to start brushing at the head and then work your way down the back to the tail. The sides should follow, finishing with the legs. Use short, quick strokes, and don't press hard. While you brush, angle the bristles away from the skin so that you don't irritate it.

It is important to get your dog used to the idea of brushing. It is a strange feeling to a dog and can stress him out if he is the nervous type. Begin gradually if your dog seems unacquainted with the idea.

Types of Brushes

Many kinds of brushes are available for Bulldogs, and luckily, it's not a big deal if you pick the wrong one. Some popular brushes for Bulldogs include a pliable rubber brush with

Did You Know?

Dog hair differs from human hair in a lot of ways. For example, dogs have compound hair follicles, which means that as many as 20 hairs can pop up from each pore. Human beings have only one hair per follicle. In addition, dogs have not one but three different kinds of hairs: guard hairs (longer and coarser), undercoat (soft and thick), and medium hairs. Different breeds have different concentrations of each kind, but each individual hair follicle produces all three kinds of hair, usually one guard hair and several finer hairs. Although the hair follicles are living cells, hair itself is dead, no matter what they say in shampoo commercials.

several soft spikes or nubs, the slicker brush (with flexible metal pins), and a rubber grooming mitt.

The pliable rubber brush and slicker brush will both strip out the dead hair from the coat, but the slicker is best for the undercoat, and the pliable rubber brush is best for the top coat. The grooming mitt will finish it off with a nice polish to the Bulldog's short coat.

How to Brush Your Bulldog

Begin at the back of the head, using the slicker brush with gentle, flowing strokes. The aim is to remove the dead hair and dirt from the undercoat. Then repeat with the slicker. Some groomers recommend beginning at the rear and brushing gently *against* the hair growth pattern to stimulate the skin and remove loose hair. Then brush along the hair growth pattern and follow with a rubdown or polishing with the grooming mitt. Use whatever method works best for you and your dog, but always finish by praising him like mad.

BATHING

A well-brushed dog doesn't need a daily bath, but most people err on the side of bathing their dogs less often than they should. Bathing your dog correctly with a high-quality dog shampoo with conditioner will not strip away his natural oils any more than washing your hair every day does yours. In fact, a buildup of these oils can give your dog a pretty heady odour, so bathe your Bulldog as often as you find necessary. Bathing keeps your dog clean and is a great prevention against hot spots.

You can bathe your Bulldog in the bath or utility sink—in fact, anywhere that you have a supply of warm water and can restrain your dog. If you use a bath, put down a rubber mat; enamel is slippery stuff, and your dog could slide and injure himself. Baths are also a real strain on the back. If your shower doesn't have a hand-held spray attachment, get one. This inexpensive, easily installed device will pay for itself in terms of comfort the very first time you use it. You might also consider using a mesh drain liner for collecting all that pesky hair that falls out.

Supplies

Before beginning, gather your supplies. A tearless shampoo for dogs or humans is best. You can even buy canine shampoos and rinses designed especially for the colour of your dog (red, white,

Grooming Supplies

The following grooming supplies will keep your Bulldog healthy and looking his best.

- Brushes
- Shampoo
- Cotton-tip applicators and cotton balls
- Baby powder
- Mustard squirt bottle (clean and empty, of course) to squirt cleaner into the hard-to-access wrinkles, especially under the nose rope
- Nail clippers or a grinder
- Canine toothbrush and toothpaste
- Grooming table (while not a necessity, it may come in handy)

etc.) at grooming shops, pet supply shops, and dog shows. You should also have some cotton balls, cotton-tipped swabs, and mineral oil or eye ointment. Put a drop of this in the eyes before you begin; it will help keep out the shampoo. Also, place cotton in the dog's ears to keep water from running in them.

How to Bathe Your Bulldog

Soak the dog completely, up and down, front and back. Dogs hate hot water, so make the bath water lukewarm. That's warm enough to get him clean and cool enough so he won't complain, at least not too much. Start at the neck and work backward, making sure not to miss the areas between the toes, under the tail, and the genitals. You can also wash the face gently with a washcloth and a bit of shampoo. You must take special care of the Bulldog's wrinkles and tail pocket! Then wash the nose and outside of the ears.

Follow with a conditioner rinse if desired. Then rinse like mad, especially around those wrinkles—you don't want soap drying in there and irritating the skin. It should take twice as long to rinse the dog as it did to wash him. Then rinse him again. Towel dry, and clean the inside of the ears with a washcloth after you take out the cotton balls. You can also let your dog air dry at this point, or use a hair dryer designed for dogs, being careful not to use one around

To bathe your Bulldog, soak him with lukewarm water and shampoo him all over.

the head. (Some human ones are too hot.) Keep the dog inside until he's dry. (This may take a couple of hours.) Make sure the wrinkles get dry, too! Wet wrinkles can lead to infection.

WRINKLE CARE

Bulldog wrinkles need frequent cleaning. They are prone to irritation and can collect dirt and debris. It's not enough to clean them only when you're bathing the dog. The older Bulldogs get, the more they tend to wrinkle, so you'll need to step it up as your pet ages. You can't go wrong by washing those wrinkles every day at the same time you brush his teeth. Hot, humid weather causes more trouble because it produces conditions that allow bacteria to accumulate.

Depending on the condition of the wrinkles, you can use a cloth with plain water or you can add a bit of baby shampoo. An easier solution is to use baby wipes with aloe and lanolin. Try squirting the cleansing material into the wrinkle with a clean plastic mustard squeezer. The nose wrinkle needs special attention; if it looks irritated, use a soothing cream or ointment. You can apply the ointment with a child's toothbrush.

TEAR STAINS (EPIPHORA)

Some dogs do not have proper tear drainage. This can result from clogged lacrimal ducts, or more commonly, a conformation that prevents the tears from opening the duct. It can also occur because the tears that are produced are too thick to flow into the duct opening.

Reddish-brown tear stains occur most noticeably on dogs with light-coloured coats and heavy wrinkles. The colour is due to normal facial bacteria mixing with the tears. In pronounced cases, a crust forms in the corner of the eye and over the skin, sometimes even resulting in small ulcers. Some stains are just the result of hair near the eyes absorbing moisture from the eyes. Other stains are related to diet, health, and genetics. (Mother dogs with tear stains are likely to have offspring with the same problem.) The damp, heavily wrinkled face of a Bulldog provides a good ground for the growth of bacteria and yeast, including the infamous "red yeast," which not only looks bad but smells bad, too. The red yeast can even infect the tear ducts, which increases the problem. Unless the tear staining comes from a clogged tear duct, there's really nothing that can be done to prevent it from occurring.

Tear stains present a special grooming challenge. To do the most effective job, try to determine the source. (You may need a

Clean your Bulldog's wrinkles daily to remove dirt and debris that may gather there.

veterinarian's advice.) Some commercial products are available, and you can also try to bleach the stains out with a mixture of 1 tablespoon of hydrogen peroxide, a little milk of magnesia, and enough cornstarch to make a paste. Other people have had success with a boric acid ointment. Spread the stuff on top of the stain; you should see the stain disappear or at least lighten up after several weeks. Take care not to get anything in the dog's eyes.

Some people have actually consulted veterinary ophthalmologists for recalcitrant cases, and to help some animals, have opted for eye duct surgery that increases tear capacity.

NAIL CARE

Keep your Bulldog's nails in good repair. This means that you should clip them every other week or so, less often if your Bulldog walks a lot on hard pavement. Keep your Bulldog's nails trimmed short enough so that they don't touch the floor when he walks. Long nails can eventually lead to a deformed foot. If the nails are very hard, soak them in warm water for 15 minutes before you begin.

Types of Clippers

Use good quality canine (not human) nail clippers, either a scissor or guillotine type. Either kind of clipper works fine as long as you keep the equipment sharp. Dull blades don't work, and they will hurt your dog. Human toenail clippers aren't strong or sharp enough for canine nails. Most groomers consider the guillotine-type clippers the best and easiest to operate. However, if your Bulldog tends to have cracked nails, a guillotine-type clipper can crush them. Scissors-type clippers tend to be stronger and sharper, and it's easier, in my experience, to estimate where the quick of the nail is.

You can also use an electric nail grinder. Some dogs may prefer a grinder once they get used to the noise. You just need to watch that the grinder doesn't get too hot.

How to Clip Your Bulldog's Nails

Nail clipping can be stressful for both the Bulldog and his owner. Owners worry about clipping the nails too short, and their fear is translated to the dog. Try to make this experience as pleasant as possible for the dog. To do this right, you'll need to control him, something that's best accomplished with a grooming table, although some people sit right on the floor with their dogs. You may need an assistant, especially at first, because many Bulldogs simply detest having their nails done. Try distracting your Bulldog with a bit of peanut butter or other chewy treat while you're grooming him to take his mind off the process. If you don't make too big a deal of it, he won't either.

When clipping, avoid the quick, which is the live part of the nail. You can easily see the quick on a white-nailed dog, but if your dog has black nails, just cut to the curve. (If the nails are very long, you'll have to do only a little bit at a time, since the quick will continue to grow longer and longer.) To trim your puppy's nails, hold one rear paw in one hand firmly but without squeezing. (Most dogs are less fussy about their rear paws, so it's often easier to begin with one of them.) Press lightly enough to separate the toes, and clip each nail right below the quick. That's the part that hurts. If you leave any ragged edges, a touch with a nail file will polish

Your Bulldog's nails should be clipped every other week if he does not wear them down naturally on pavement

the nails off nicely. If you happen to clip a nail too short, simply apply some styptic powder to the nail to stem bleeding. Just take a pinch of it between your thumb and forefinger and press against the cut nail. If you're caught without any powder, you can try using a little cornstarch or flour in the same manner. Don't make a big deal of it.

The pads of the feet also deserve care. As tough as they appear, they can be torn, caked with tar, or embedded with thorns. Trim the hair between the pads, also. Long hair can become caked with gunk and form an impenetrable mass that is painful to your dog. In serious cases, a foot infection could develop. Tar can be removed from paw pads by applying petroleum jelly or mineral oil to the affected area. Follow with warm water and a mild soap. Never use turpentine or paint thinner to remove tar.

NOSE CARE

The Bulldog's nose tends to dry out. Fix it by smearing some petroleum jelly on the nose regularly.

TAIL CARE

Some Bulldogs have their tail set in a "pocket." If this is the case with your dog, you'll need to clean the pocket often since all kinds of debris can accumulate in there. Apply an ointment or powder when finished.

DENTAL CARE

As you might expect, the Bulldog's mouth is pretty important. Dogs need a mouth to eat, drink, groom themselves, cool off, and communicate. It's up to you to take good care of it!

Dog teeth are subject to the same dental problems we humans have: plaque, tartar, and gum and tooth disease. Plaque is the sticky stuff that covers the teeth. It's a delightful mix of bacteria, saliva, food particles, and dead cells from the mouth lining. It is constantly deposited on the teeth and gums and can harden into tartar in less than two days. Once tartar forms, it makes a structure to let even more plaque accumulate, and so on. It's a vicious cycle for sure, and one that leads to periodontal disease. Fortunately, preventing periodontal disease is as simple as brushing your dog's teeth every day.

You should brush your dog's teeth about as often as you brush your own. It takes about the same length of time. Not only is it healthy and a way to bond with your dog, it's also a good chance for you to carefully examine your Bulldog's mouth every day for tartar buildup, swellings, and broken teeth. It's amazing what you may find in there. When you brush your dog's teeth properly, you are removing plaque in the groove below the gum line where chew toys and doggy treats don't reach. You can also rinse your dog's mouth with an oral rinse, or you can use dental wipes every day.

To accustom your dog to having his teeth brushed, start by putting a little of the canine toothpaste on your finger and just letting him lick it. Soon you'll be able to run your finger, perhaps covered with a bit of soft cloth, around his teeth. In no time at all, you can graduate to a toothbrush!

Dogs can get cavities, but they are relatively rare. The cause is usually a high-sugar diet, so lay off the sugary snacks. You will also need to take your Bulldog for a regular professional dental cleaning. The vet will anaesthetise him, flush out the mouth, and clean the teeth with both hand-held and ultrasonic scalers to remove all tartar from above and below the gum line. She will polish the teeth as well—not because it makes them whiter, but because polishing removes microscopic scratches on the teeth that make a good home for plaque and tartar buildup. You can slightly reduce your dog's chances of developing dental disease by feeding a hard kibble diet. Certain dog chews and toys may also help remove plaque, but they do not replace daily tooth brushing.

A dog's mouth is subject to the same problems that humans have, so it's important to inspect it frequently for signs of disease.

TRAINING *and* BEHAVIOUR
of Your Bulldog

Bulldogs respond well only to positive training. These are independent, smart dogs who do not blossom under punishment or harsh treatment of any kind. Their tough exterior hides a tender soul. They also respond best in a situation when trust has been established between them and their owners. Positive training may not be the fastest way to get the results you want, but it's the best way because you will build rather than damage your relationship.

The earlier you start training your dog, the better, as young dogs have fewer bad habits to overcome. You should concentrate your first training efforts on building trust. For your Bulldog to have the best learning experience possible, you need to create a safe environment. Focus on praise rather than punishment, and view the training process as teaching. Don't expect your Bulldog to turn into Rin Tin Tin, though. This is not an "obedience breed," and your Bulldog is not going to wait breathlessly while you tell him what to do. Figure out what you really want him to learn and then proceed slowly, making sure he has achieved one skill before advancing to the next.

To get the most positive response from your Bulldog, try to figure out what motivates him most. It might be food, play, or praise. Just remember that your Bulldog is an individual who will respond in a unique way to training. In addition, reward a desired behaviour the second it occurs, not five minutes later. Bulldogs live in the now.

While dogs understand many more everyday words than we previously thought, they are more attuned to your tone of voice than to your vocabulary. Your tone should match your meaning. If you praise your dog in a dark or unhappy tone of voice, he won't get the message. If you scold him in a cheerful way, he won't get that, either.

SOCIALISATION

If your puppy is between 4 and 12 months old, he is in the socialisation period, his once-in-a-lifetime opportunity to learn how to play well with others and respond positively to new things. If you fail to take advantage of this period, it's very possible that your dog will be doomed to an antisocial, fearful life.

Around the middle of this period is the so-called fear period, the time where in the wild, the pups would first leave their dens to encounter the world. It was a dangerous world, so puppies developed a cautious attitude toward its exploration. Today, puppies have the same cautious instincts, so it is very important during this time for your Bulldog to have as few fearful experiences as possible. These negative experiences can become embedded in his psyche.

To this end, it's wise to introduce your pup to new things only gradually. Let him meet other dogs and people a few at a time. Don't just plunge him into a large group of strangers. You know your pup best, so gauge by his attitude how ready he is to expand his horizons. Your Bulldog's adventures might include puppy kindergarten, puppy play groups, your friends' houses, and pet shops.

If your dog seems confident, introduce him in a positive way to nail clippers, the vacuum cleaner, hair dryer, and air-conditioning unit. If he learns that noise doesn't equal pain, he'll feel more secure. In addition, take your Bulldog on walks so that he can encounter people of every age, dress, race, and accoutrement, including wheelchairs, canes, and walkers. Babies, children, people in uniform, and people with beards and hats should certainly be part of the routine as well.

Clicker Training

One popular way to train dogs uses a method called "clicker training." Clicker training is a form of operant conditioning using a clicker as a marker to help your dog identify a behaviour that produces a reward (usually small treats). In clicker training, you don't give a command until after a behaviour is reliably repeated. You use the clicker to "capture" the correct behaviour.

HOUSETRAINING

Puppies will have accidents, just like kids do. Humans are supposed to be smarter than dogs, but many children are often not toilet trained until the age of three—yet some owners expect their puppy to be perfect at four months! If you change those unrealistic expectations, you'll save yourself a lot of grief.

If you're oblivious to what's going on until your puppy actually starts relieving himself, don't panic. It's not the end of the world. If you start screaming, you'll convince your dog that he has done something awful (not that relieving himself in the house is awful, but that toileting altogether is awful). Because your Bulldog can't stop relieving himself, he'll start hiding it. The key is to act calmly and to promptly teach the puppy the nuanced lesson that toileting *outside* is award-winning; toileting inside is nonrewarding.

To socialise your Bulldog puppy, gradually introduce him to new dogs and people.

Keys to Successful Housetraining

The keys to successful housetraining include:

- Containment
- Attention
- Reward
- Patience
- Scheduling

Containment

Containment is synonymous with crating your Bulldog. Should you use a crate? In a word, yes. A crate is you and your dog's best friend. Containment is the essence of housetraining, but it should be used in moderation. First of all, forcing a dog to stay in a crate too long defeats the very purpose of crate training. After all, he can only hold it so long, and if left in a crate for an extended period of time, your poor Bulldog will be forced to urinate in it. This, in turn, breaks down the natural inhibitions he has about urinating in his den. Before long, you'll have more problems than before.

Practise putting your puppy in the crate for brief periods when you are home with him. Give him a toy or snack to work on while he's there. This will help him associate the crate with a pleasant place to be.

It's a dog world axiom that a puppy up to eight months of age can "hold it" as many hours as his age in months, plus one. Thus, a two-month-old puppy should be able hold it for three hours. However, puppies need plenty of exercise and opportunities to explore their surroundings. The idea of keeping an eight-month-old dog in a crate all day is repulsive. Even if your Bulldog somehow valiantly manages to hang on longer than is good for him, you may be courting future disasters in the form of bladder stones.

I believe that four hours is the maximum time a dog should be left in a crate. There is more to consider here than whether or not the dog will urinate in the house. You need to consider his psychological needs and his need for exercise. Dogs are complex creatures, and the highly intelligent, curious Bulldog cannot bear the attendant psychological deprivation that naturally goes along with long periods of being crated.

If you must keep your dog in a crate for longer periods of time, be absolutely sure to exercise him before and after his period of confinement. If this means getting up earlier in the morning to go for a walk with your Bulldog, please do so. If you must be gone for longer periods, please help your dog by hiring a dog walker to take care of his potty needs.

Reward

When your puppy succeeds in accomplishing his mission, praise him lavishly. A sedate pat on the head and a "Good boy, Warren!" won't suffice. Go crazy with joy and exuberant praise. If you have time, let him play a bit before you bring him inside. This will act as a further reward. If you take him directly inside afterward, he'll respond by delaying the precipitating event as long as possible outside, since he's undoubtedly enjoying himself

Attention

One mark of the astute dog owner is figuring out the signs of impending toileting. While the puppy is still learning how to tell you he wants to go, it's up to you to figure it out on your own. Can you do it? Are you smarter than your Bulldog?

Common signs of an upcoming event include circling the floor, paw or mouth licking, and whining. The last behaviour is

Did You Know?

You're doing your Bulldog a great favour if you enrol him in an elementary training or socialisation class. Look for one that operates using rewards rather than punishment. Not only will your Bulldog learn manners, but more importantly, you'll learn a few things yourself. This is also a great opportunity for you to bond with your dog. You can usually enter your puppy at three months, with "graduation" at five months. These classes are valuable because they help your puppy develop socialisation skills with people and other dogs.

especially useful, and one you want to encourage, because you don't have to be in the same room as your dog to get the signal.

Often, puppies don't think of relieving themselves until it's an emergency situation, so you may want to simply pick up your dog and carry him out. This will prevent an accident happening on the way to the door, a fairly common occurrence.

Patience

Be patient. Your Bulldog puppy has a tiny bladder and almost no bladder or anal sphincter control, and he won't have control until he is at least four months old. When you put these two factors together, it soon becomes clear that puppy housetraining is a job that requires your constant attention. But take my word for it—if you do everything (or even most things) correctly in the beginning, the entire process will not take long. Remember that you are dealing with an intelligent and eager-to-please pet. If you do your part and make it clear what you want, your Bulldog will do his part. A puppy is housetrained when he knows what you want and makes every effort to comply. Simply because he can't wait as long as an older dog doesn't mean he's not trained; it means he has reached his limit.

Scheduling

Keep to a schedule. Eight-week-old puppies should go out every couple of hours. Puppies new to the household should go out even more frequently, as nervousness and excitement stimulate their bladders. Most adult dogs can be left alone for eight hours, but this is variable, just as it is with people. Don't leave food out in a dish all day long for your unhousetrained dog; it can mess up his schedule.

When your Bulldog understands that he can depend on you to take him out at regular times (dogs have clocks in their heads), he'll be more inclined to wait for that moment. If he doesn't have a clue when or if you're going to take him out, he may feel as if he has nothing to wait for.

A strict schedule should apply to eating times as well, because the two events—eating and toileting—are connected. If you have to leave your dog alone all day and he can't hold it, think about hiring a dog-walking or pet-sitting service. Or take some of that unused holiday time. Your Bulldog will appreciate the company, too.

It's best to select a particular spot you want your Bulldog to use as his private bathroom. You can reduce lawn stains that way, and also reduce the chances you yourself will step in something unpleasant.

How to Housetrain Your Bulldog

In order to successfully housetrain your Bulldog puppy, you must go outside with him. Do not just let him out to wander around aimlessly in the garden. If you do that, you won't know whether he has succeeded in his mission or not. If left outside on his own, your puppy will undoubtedly find it so interesting and exciting that he'll completely forget why he is outdoors in the first place. A less adventuresome puppy may simply sit down on the back steps and wait for you to join him. He'd rather be with you, anyway, and you accompanying him will make his outdoor duty seem less like an exile and more like a walk. But it isn't a walk. Don't allow him to toddle off everywhere smelling everything; keep him focused. I find it helps to encourage the puppy to walk in circles in the area you have selected as his bathroom. Praise him when he succeeds.

If you cannot teach your Bulldog to bark when he wants in or out, you can buy a doggie doorbell designed to prevent scratching. A pad can be placed on either side of your door at your dog's height. When your pet touches the pad, a built-in wireless transmitter will activate a door chime. You can also install a pet door. Other owners train their dogs to come and sit in front of them when they wish to go out.

When Accidents Happen

If an accident does occur, assume it *is* an accident, and don't go ballistic or scold your puppy. If you're too late to catch him, clean it up and forget about it. Your dog certainly has! Just try to be more attentive next time.

When cleaning, use enzyme cleaners that will neutralise the scent. It's usually best to clean up the mess out of sight of the puppy. Never rub your Bulldog's nose in his excrement; this is a form of punishment that is dirty, cruel, and ineffective. And of

On hot summer days, your Bulldog will need to drink more water, and as a result, he'll need to go out more frequently. Don't take away his water dish in the hopes that he won't need to urinate as much. You'll succeed only in tormenting the poor creature with thirst. However, feeding your dog dry food rather than tinned food will reduce his need to urinate frequently.

course, you should never strike your Bulldog for any reason, least of all for a household accident. Doing so will only make him afraid of you and will do nothing to change the behaviour.

Scolding your puppy after the fact only confuses him. He'll assume you are scolding him for relieving himself altogether, not for relieving himself in the wrong place. Since he can't stop himself from relieving himself, he'll be forced to find secret little places to accomplish his mission. Then you'll be wandering all around the house, wrinkling your nose and exclaiming, "I *know* there's an accident around here somewhere…where is it?"

I also have a suspicion that scolding a dog for toileting inappropriately encourages him to start eating the evidence itself. If this occurs, you'll have not one but two unfortunate habits to discourage. Some dogs acquire this awful habit (called coprophagia) anyway, but scolding a dog for a housetraining mistake can be a factor in producing it, especially in cases where dogs consume their *own* faeces.

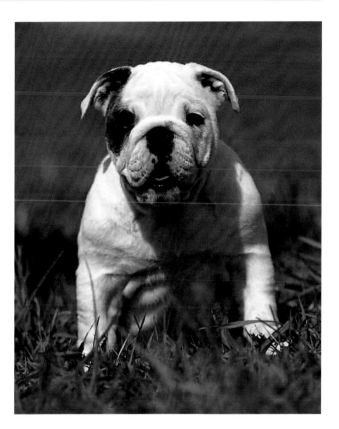

Keeping your puppy focused on the task at hand will help him become housetrained more quickly.

Correcting a Mistake

If you catch your Bulldog in the act (not afterward), grab a lead (you should have several, one hanging on each available doorknob), and cry, "Out, out!" Then race outside with him and praise him for finishing outdoors. If you actually pick up the puppy, he will probably stop peeing while you're en route, but I can't guarantee it.

Cleaning Up

If the accident occurs on a rug, use an enzyme cleaner and follow the directions on the label. Unfortunately, if you try to clean the spot with a more conventional cleaner first, the enzyme cleaner will not be as effective

Some people tout the advantages of household vinegar for cleaning up urine. This works very well if you don't mind a spot smelling of dog pee and vinegar. In reality, vinegar does not remove dog urine odours from carpet. Your best bet is one of the newer enzyme cleaners on the market that really do work. Never use an ammonia-based cleaner to remove a dog urine stain. Because ammonia smells like urine to a dog, you'll only succeed in making him think that that spot is a good place to relieve himself.

When Urination Is More Than Just Urination

Unlike human beings (at least unlike most civilised human beings), dogs have discovered a use for urination that goes far beyond simple toileting. This is what I call the urination subtext. It's up to you as the more intelligent mammal to figure out what your Bulldog is trying to tell you when he relieves himself.

Submissive Urination

This is a commonly observed behaviour in rescued dogs, shy dogs, puppies, and in new dogs introduced into a household where there are dominant dogs. Not all house soiling is the result of incomplete housetraining. When submissive urination occurs, a shy dog is responding to perceived threats by urinating on the floor. The key here is "perceived threat." *You* may think you are just "disciplining" your dog, but he figures that you are trying to hurt him. Some dogs are so submissive that they urinate even when a person just approaches them. In some cases, the dog crouches or even rolls over on his back while urinating. What you are seeing is fear, pure and simple.

Submissive urination is a natural action. Wild dogs urinate submissively before pack leaders. Unfortunately, while submissive urination has a mollifying effect on the canine pack leader, it usually leads to the opposite response in human owners, who become even angrier. Then the dog thinks, "Hmm, my owner must not have seen me urinate. I'd better do it again." This is the kind of miscommunication that can lead to real trouble.

Consider a Litter Box

Even though we have become accustomed to thinking that dogs have to relieve themselves outdoors, most of us have been surprised by enough presents on the floor to know that dogs don't always share our point of view.

In some cases, a litter box can be the perfect answer to housetraining woes. Here are some examples:

- When you live 10 storeys up and you can't face dragging your Bulldog outside at 3:00 a.m.
- When either you or your dog is ill, old, or arthritic, and the daily outside voyage is a little too much.
- When you're going to be gone for hours and you know it's not fair to ask the dog to "hold it."

Canine litter trays are on the market now, so all you have to do is teach your dog to use one. Line the litter box with something similar to the surface your dog is used to. If it's tarmac, you may have a problem, but you can substitute a clay-based litter.

Introduce your dog to the litter tray at times when he's most likely to need it, like after waking up or after meals. If you're lucky, he'll use it immediately and you can go wild with praise. Even some curious sniffing around the tray is worth some verbal encouragement from you. You can also try taking the litter tray outside with you and encouraging your Bulldog to use it out there. When he gets the idea, start bringing the tray closer to the house until he's litter trained.

Luckily, the solution for submissive urination is simple: Stop punishing the dog. Instead of penalising negative actions, reward positive behaviour. If your dog is a submissive urinator, ignore the action completely. Don't scold, glare, yell, strike him, or even call attention to the fact that he urinated. Instead, ignore the mess, walk out of the room, and clean it up later. Specifically, avoid eye contact with the miscreant. Dogs regard eye contact as either a threat, or in sophisticated dogs, as a reward—and you don't want to give either message! The less attention your Bulldog receives in response to his behaviour, the less likely he will be to repeat it. It may take a while, but gradually your submissive dog will acquire the self-confidence to rid himself of the habit.

To avoid submissive urination, keep your greetings to the dog low key. Approach from the side rather than from the front. Don't tower over him any more than you can help until he regains some confidence. Crouch down, lean back, open your arms, and call the dog to you. Avoid looking directly into his eyes. Stroke him on the chest or under the chin, not on the top of the head. When he responds with positive, assured actions, pet and play with him. Remember that dogs who submissively urinate have self-confidence problems, and these dogs should never be punished.

Territorial Marking

Unneutered males often develop the unpleasant habit of marking their territory by lifting their leg and urinating on walls or furniture. This may be more likely to occur if there's another dog around, either a female in heat or a male the unneutered male perceives as a challenge. (Even dogs who don't mark in their homes almost certainly will do so outside.) When a dog marks, he releases only a small amount of urine (as opposed to regular urination).

Neutered males may also exhibit this behaviour, although less frequently. I have even observed this behaviour (although usually outdoors) in dominant females. It may also crop up if there has been a change in family structure and the dominant partner leaves. In a few cases, insecure or anxious dogs will also mark, perhaps feeling that it empowers them. Marking is due to the presence of the testosterone hormone.

To a lesser extent, the same behaviour applies to defecation. I have seen many an unneutered male defecate directly in front of a rival, especially when the latter was penned up and unable to retaliate.

If your house marker is not neutered, the best cure is to have him neutered as soon as you can. If that is not possible, treat the marking problem the same as you would a regular housetraining lapse. Say, "No," and get the dog outside immediately. Older, more confident dogs may be firmly scolded.

Exuberant or Excitement Urination

Sometimes your puppy is so excited to see you that he just can't hold it another instant. This behaviour is not really

When It's Time to See the Vet

If your Bulldog relieves himself in a way you think isn't normal—too much, too little, odd posture, straining or discomfort, or odd places or circumstances—take him to your vet first for a thorough exam. All kinds of medical conditions could cause the problem.

Certain medical conditions manifest themselves by increased urination, urinary incontinence, or difficulty urinating. Elderly females often "leak," especially at night while sleeping. Cushing's disease, bladder stones, chronic kidney failure, brain or spinal cord injury, diabetes, and certain medications can all affect urination patterns.

If you notice any changes or abnormalities in your Bulldog's toileting habits, note them carefully and consult your veterinarian. Bring a sample to the surgery with you if possible.

Lavishly praise your Bulldog when he executes a training command well.

related to submissive urination, although at first glance they may seem similar. However, a dog who experiences excitement urination doesn't crouch or act submissive. He's just thrilled. It occurs mostly at playtime and is characteristic of dogs under one year of age. These dogs become so involved with their activity that they just can't hold it any longer. This problem usually disappears on its own as the dog gains more control over his natural functions.

The cure for excitement urination is much the same as for submissive urination. The best way to react to this behaviour is not to react at all. If you return your Bulldog's jubilant greeting too enthusiastically, he won't receive the correct message. Be calm, nonchalant even, as you greet your dog. Walk into another room and examine your post. In a few minutes, after the dog is a little calmer, you may pet him and greet him. Then take him outside to relieve himself.

BASIC TRAINING

Modern dogs need to be mannerly household pets and citizens of the world. A trained dog is a pleasure to be around and will be included more often in activities than will an ill-trained dog. Good training can also save your dog's life.

There is a difference between general good behaviour around the house and formal obedience. Many dogs are a joy to have

Keep initial training sessions short and fun— your Bulldog will enjoy them more!

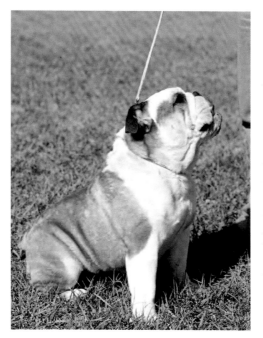

around the house, even though they can't fetch or heel. Bulldogs are much better (usually) at being well mannered than well trained. However, it's certainly not impossible to train your Bulldog to perform routine commands like sitting, lying down, and heeling.

One way to make your training more successful is to make use of "treats," "bait," or "lures," different names for the same thing. When you are first teaching a particular skill to your dog, use a treat every time. As your Bulldog learns what you want of him, you can start handing out treats more infrequently—not every time. Studies show that animals actually learn better when rewards are offered intermittently, after they understand what is desired of them.

All first training sessions should be indoors, where there are fewer distractions.

Watch Me

This is the basic focus command. If your dog isn't paying any attention to you, he won't be able to learn anything. Help him focus by using positive reinforcement and treats. This doesn't mean that you should give your dog food every time he looks at you. It means that he should always consider it as a viable possibility. Once he learns that "watch me!" brings praise or even a reward, he'll be anxious to learn what you have to say next.

To teach "watch me!" say the words and hold a treat near your face. If your Bulldog doesn't see the treat at first, you may have to start to lower it toward his field of vision. He'll catch on soon.

The number of times you do anything should depend on the age, training, and maturity of your Bulldog. Stop while he is still having fun! Usually a minute or two is long enough.

Leave It

This simple command is a lifesaver. Young dogs are forever getting into rubbish, nappies, and expensive shoes. Start teaching your Bulldog by waiting until he is chewing on an object that he really doesn't care that much about. (It should also be one that's not important to you, either.) As he's chewing, go up to your dog, and say, "Leave it!" Offer him a treat in exchange. Make sure the treat is preferable to what he's chewing. Bits of bacon and cheese are great favourites. Praise him when he accepts the exchange.

In real life, you would be most likely to use this command when the dog has found something truly heady like a rabbit carcass, so your established reward needs to be very powerful. A normal Bulldog won't trade a rotting carcass for a dry dog biscuit. Of course, you probably won't have any bacon actually on hand when the infraction occurs, but it's okay to cheat that one time. Afterward, practise "leave it" several more times with your accustomed treat and plenty of praise.

Sit

To teach your dog the sit, first grab a few pieces of tiny treats. Treats are absolutely essential. It's also important that you remember never to try to force your Bulldog to sit. Hold the treat *at your puppy's nose level*. Practise in a corner where he can't back up. As he extends his neck toward the treat, move your hand slowly over the top of his head (not too high) and back, saying, "Sit." Most dogs will automatically move into a sit in order to retrieve the treat. Give him the treat the instant he sits, and praise him enthusiastically. Practise several times, but keep the training session very short when puppies are involved. Five minutes is plenty of time for both you and your Bulldog.

Do not force your dog to complete this exercise; encourage him, and reward him with praise and a treat. Nothing about the training should be forced or painful. If your dog gets up too quickly, refrain from treating him. He needs to learn that the treat comes only when he is actually sitting. Otherwise, you'll turn him into a jack-in-the-box. You should have all of your family members perform this exercise until everyone knows the drill.

Basic Equipment

You can't train your dog without a few basic pieces of equipment. They include a buckle collar, lead, and treats. The need for additional equipment depends on what you're training your dog to do. If you are teaching your Bulldog to fetch, you'll need a ball. If you're teaching him to jump through a hoop, you'll need a hoop. The most important piece of equipment, though, is a good attitude on your part. This includes patience and a positive but realistic attitude about what you expect your Bulldog to do.

Teach your Bulldog to sit before he eats, before he goes out the door, or before any exciting activity. This will give him an opportunity to calm down, and it will give you an opportunity to keep in control (and go out first).

Down

This is the next logical command after the sit. Most dogs rather dislike being asked to lie down, although they are happy enough to do it on their own. This is because the down puts them in a vulnerable position, both physically and psychologically.

To teach the down, use the treat method again. While the dog is sitting, lower the treat slowly and move it between his front legs toward the floor. Most dogs will lie down naturally. If yours doesn't after a few tries, you can gently extend his front legs and praise him as you ease him to the floor. Practise a few times before moving on to something else. Don't try to force him down. You want your dog to perform joyfully, not out of fear or pain.

Teach stay by saying the word and then slowly retreating.

In formal obedience classes, your Bulldog may learn a long down-stay, which usually lasts for several minutes. This command is simply a combination of down and stay. Bulldogs can be pretty good at this. Sometimes they even fall asleep!

Stay

Although some people teach the stay as a separate command, I prefer to use the sit, which means that my dog should sit until I say, "Okay!" I believe that teaching the stay as a separate command is confusing to dogs, because you're not asking them to do anything new—you're just asking them to keep doing what you have already asked them to do. However, other people believe that saying, "Stay" signals to the dog early that he'll be sitting for quite some time. At any rate, never ask your dog to sit-stay for more than a few seconds when you are starting out. You want to make success easy for him.

Teach stay by saying the word and gradually and slowly retreating. Reward him for remaining in one place.

Again, quit while the training is still fun. The length of time you teach this command depends on your individual dog, but five minutes is usually long enough.

Stand

The stand is a very important command for dogs to learn. After all, dogs stand while they are being bathed, groomed, and examined by the vet. Show dogs stand in the show ring. To teach this command, get out your trusty "lure" or "bait." Slowly raise the treat to where his nose would be if he were standing. Very soon he will "stand." At first you may have to hold him up and keep the treat a few inches in front of his nose so that he stretches to get it, but then he will soon catch on that he can stand and nibble the treat while it is still in your hand.

Come

Although teaching your Bulldog to respond to your command to come is the most important lesson of all, sometimes it can be very difficult. Bulldogs, while anxious to please, are rather adamant about having their own way. As a result, the best plan is to make your wishes and your Bulldog's wishes one and the same. You must make him realise that you are the source of the treats, the pets, the praise, and the fun.

Never call your Bulldog for anything unpleasant, such as punishment, baths, or medication. When you have to give your dog a pill, you'll need to go after him yourself.

To encourage your Bulldog to come, you must make yourself the most enchanting object there is. Start indoors in a small room when your dog is young and most dependent upon you. Call him gently and offer a treat. Chances are he'll toddle over. Praise him with every step. If he doesn't come, gently draw the lead toward you while still encouraging him. Don't jerk on it. The purpose of the lead is to help him focus. You don't want your Bulldog to get the idea that it's even thinkable to go in a different direction than the one you're calling him to. When he responds by taking some steps in the right direction, praise him. When he reaches you, treat him. If he seems reluctant, try kneeling down so you are at the same level. This gives him confidence. Lean back and open your

Come Tip

You want your Bulldog to associate the come command with pleasant things. Never use come to call your dog for anything unpleasant, like baths, trips to the vet, or medication.

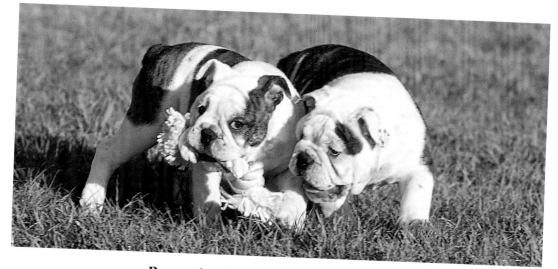

Possession Aggression

If your Bulldog is possessive-aggressive of a particular toy, try trading it for an even better treat.

This unacceptable behaviour pattern begins in puppyhood. In fact, it's unlikely that a dog who has never shown aggressiveness over food or toys will suddenly begin doing so as an adult. Dogs demonstrating this behaviour pattern will stand over their toy or food bowl and stare hard at anyone who approaches. In cases of food aggression, they will stop eating. The staring may be accompanied by growls, snapping, or biting. Obviously, this is something you'll need to nip in the bud.

First, you must realise that such behaviour is actually quite natural. Dogs naturally wish to hang on to favoured items, and in the wild, they know that if they give up their bone to another animal, they won't eat that day. However, even in the wild, dogs will surrender a meal to the dominant member of the pack. In your household, that's you. This is the way it should be in your home: You and all other human beings are the "top dog." Dogs aren't born seeing it that way, though; it's something they need to be taught. However, you don't teach them by snatching their food or toys away. That only confirms their suspicion that you are not their friend.

In order for dogs to overcome possession aggression, they first need to realise that they are in no danger of having their food permanently removed. When approaching a dog who seems to be guarding a treat, dog bowl, or toy, try trading that desirable item for an even more desirable item with him. For example, if he's eating kibble, he'll be happy to come over for a piece of cheese. In more serious cases, you may have to avoid giving him long-lasting chewing treats altogether, at least for a while. Give him only small biscuits he can devour at once without "owning" them. And in established cases of food aggression, it's wise to start by taking away your dog's food bowl completely and feeding him by hand until he becomes used to the basic idea that all food comes from you. If your dog seems suspicious of your approach, drop a tender morsel of food in the bowl every time he eats.

In less serious cases, it helps to keep the food bowl in a big, empty space rather than in a corner that's easier to protect. Don't give the dog his "special corner" in which to eat, either. Instead, move the bowl around and remove it immediately after the dog has eaten. Stay in the room while your Bulldog eats. This reinforces the idea that you still have control over his food. In addition, teach your Bulldog to sit and wait before you place his food bowl before him. If possible, teach him to wait until you give him permission to eat. Reward him for obeying by feeding him something better than what is in the bowl. (Let him know you have it first, or he'll wolf down the entire meal before you dig the piece of cheese out of your pocket.)

Some dogs take to "guarding" their owners, growling or snapping at the approach of other dogs or people. While most flattered owners assume the dog is protecting them, think again. What he's actually doing is guarding you—treating you like a favourite piece of rawhide. Don't be flattered. The dog is telling everyone, including you, that he owns you. If your dog guards you inappropriately, you will need to go back to the basics in establishing your leadership over him. Even if you want your Bulldog to guard you, that behaviour should come on your initiative, not his.

Biting

Every year insurance companies shell out about large sums of money in settlements and lawsuits over biting dogs. As a rule, Bulldogs are gentle, but it's never safe to assume that your dog won't bite. Any dog, given the right (or wrong!) circumstances, will bite.

If your Bulldog has ever bitten anyone, especially for what appears to be no reason, take him to your vet for a thorough physical workup, especially if the behaviour is new or sudden. It's

Did You Know?

An enormous percentage of dog "problems" are caused by simple boredom on the part of the dog and can be solved merely by giving him more exercise, more interaction, and more attention. Before you decide your dog has a real problem behaviour, try exercising him and spending more quality time with him.

possible he has a physical ailment. For example, he may have developed cataracts or another condition that limits his vision. This could lead to misidentification of a person or a general insecurity that could produce biting. Hypothyroidism, which is common in dogs, can lead to aggression. Chronic pain, like back or spinal problems, can also lead to aggressive behaviour.

If your Bulldog is pronounced healthy, make an immediate appointment with a qualified animal behaviourist, not just any dog trainer. Most dog trainers do not have the specific background necessary to deal with aggression and can even make the problem worse by putting more pressure on the dog. Take careful notes of the circumstances under which the dog bit. Many cases of biting are limited to the biting of children or other members of the family whom the dog considers weak and of a lesser status. Most dog bites, in fact, involve family members or other people well known to the dog. This is called owner-directed aggression, and it doesn't typically come from so-called dominant dogs but from dogs who are stressed and anxious. They bite because they see biting as a sensible way to resolve conflict and keep people away.

These types of dogs bite because they have been allowed to believe that biting carries no

Handling Canine Aggression

When attempting to handle canine aggression, it's important to keep the following things in mind:

- Never provoke a situation where the dog may bite. Don't chase him, and don't attempt to pull him out of a hiding place. You're just asking for trouble
- Get your dog vet-checked for any possible physical problems.
- Enrol your dog in special obedience classes for aggressive dogs. Regular obedience classes may make a dog more anxious.
- For at least two weeks, keep your interactions with your dog down to a bare minimum; make him beg for your attention.
- Do not allow your dog on furniture, including the bed.
- Make the dog sit or lie down before feeding him.
- Give your dog twice the exercise he's getting now—outside in the garden. Working dogs are less stressed and much happier, meaning they are less apt to bite.
- If necessary, keep a soft muzzle on the dog while working with him.
- Keep small children completely away from the aggressive dog at all times unless the dog is muzzled.
- Consult your vet about possible anti-depressant medication
- Use a head halter rather than a conventional or choke collar if you can get one to fit.

negative consequences. The average biting dog is an unneutered male dog, poorly socialised, and in his early adolescence. His first victim is probably a young child. His next one might be you.

Most dogs who bite have preceded the attack with a whole bunch of warning signs, most of which were covered up or ignored. He was probably allowed to mouth and chew on human fingers when he was puppy. He may have grabbed at a child's clothes or ankles as the child ran away. He may have grabbed food out of someone's hand, or he may have growled and refused to relinquish his place on the sofa to a person. He may have snapped when someone leaned over him. It should come as no surprise whatsoever when he finally bites someone. Most people think that aggressive dogs have been abused at some point in their lives. Actually, this is not true. Most aggressive dogs have been treated with kid gloves. Most families of biting dogs are quiet, gentle people. They are truly shocked when their beloved pet shows some trace of wolf-like behaviour. They are afraid and heartbroken.

Fortunately, most of these stories can have a happy ending if the dog undergoes behaviour therapy. Behaviour therapy, sometimes combined with medications like tranquilizers and antidepressants, is usually effective in curing dog aggression as long as everyone in the family cooperates to help the dog. Most of these cases develop in the first place because the owners made errors in training their dog.

Never make excuses for a dog who bites. Telling yourself or others that he didn't mean to do it or blaming others for provoking him is putting your head in the sand. Biting is a very serious problem that can cause you to lose a lawsuit or your dog if you don't get it under control. Seek help.

Barking

Excessive barking is not a major problem in most Bulldogs, but there are exceptions. The key to handling the problem is to figure out why the dog is barking in the first place. Bulldogs usually bark to alarm their families of approaching visitors. While this is a valuable contribution to family security, praising this behaviour too much can result in the Bulldog barking at every passing leaf in hopes of gaining the same attention. The secret is simply to say, "Thanks," and reward him after he has stopped barking.

Never yell at a barking dog. If you do, you're giving him

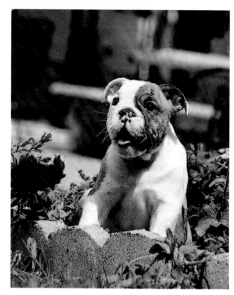

If your Bulldog tends to dig up your favourite flowers, solve the problem by giving him his own special place to dig.

attention, and dogs always bark to get some kind of attention—whether to alert you to a stranger or to call attention to his own neglected (in his eyes) state. Even negative attention like screaming at him is attention, and that's what he wants. If he's an indoor barker, ask him to sit after he has barked a few times to warn you of intruders. Then give him a treat. Dogs can't eat and bark at the same time. As I said earlier, though, barking is not a major problem with this breed.

Digging

A few Bulldogs have the unfortunate tendency to dig large, unsightly holes in the garden. However, digging a soft bed in the earth is a good way to keep cool, something that is very important to the Bulldog. Because dogs generally prefer digging in a soft spot, you might solve the problem by making your Bulldog his own earth box in a spot you have selected for him. Start him off by partially burying some favoured toys in the dirt. With any luck, he may take the hint. For best results, place the box in a spot that gets afternoon shade. If your Bulldog's favourite digging place is your petunia bed, you may have to consider enclosing it so that he may gaze in admiration but not destroy it.

It's also a very good idea to provide your Bulldog with a child's wading pool in the summer, as long as he is carefully supervised. Get one made of heavy-duty plastic, and keep it filled with cool water. At night, use the contents of the pool to water your garden. Do not punish your Bulldog for digging. He won't understand why you're doing it. Give him an alternate activity and manage the problem by supervision and attention instead.

Mouthing

Puppy mouthing is a natural but annoying practise. Puppy teeth are extremely sharp, partly to compensate for the lack of jaw power and partly to ensure the weaning process. To get your puppy to stop biting you, you need to let him know that it's inconvenient. When he bites down, cry, "Ow!" in a yelping voice, and look (or move) away. He'll soon get the idea that when he bites hard, you won't play with him. This is one way to help your puppy develop what is called bite inhibition, an especially important skill for a Bulldog, who can bite down really, really hard. That's not something you want to experience!

Pulling

Powerful dogs like Bulldogs can be strong pullers. You can handle the problem with a no-pull harness, but it's also a good idea to train your dog to stop this annoying habit.

The first step is for you to control yourself. Getting out the lead is an exciting moment, and your dog is already in "pull mode" before it is snapped on. To help him control his enthusiasm, keep calm and collected yourself. It's a good idea to practise this training for the first time *after* a walk so that you have some chance of success.

Make your Bulldog sit and stay before you attach the lead. Do not walk out the door while he is jumping around in a frenzy. He will calm down only when he realises that calm behaviour will open the door, so until he settles down, do not open the door. Let him bounce around all he wants, but don't let him walk. When he settles down, praise him. Then, take a step with him on the lead away from the door. (The door is too exciting.) If he starts jumping around, stop again. Only head for the door when he is under control. Use the same method outside. When your Bulldog pulls, stop walking. If you continue to walk, he will understand that pulling has no consequences. You can also ask him to sit for a few seconds every time he starts to pull. (Obviously, the dog needs to know how to sit first.) Soon you will have a reliable walker at your side.

Did You Know?

One common misbehaviour you will seldom see in Bulldogs is jumping up. Bulldogs like to keep all four legs on the floor. When you do have a Bulldog who jumps, simply don't give him the reward he is looking for — attention from you. Turn your back and walk away. He will soon stop.

Chewing

Destructive chewing is both annoying and dangerous. Powerful Bulldog jaws can turn your furniture into matchsticks and your carpet into shreds. Bulldogs can devour linoleum and bend forks. They can even chew through tins.

All dogs need to chew, so this is not a behaviour we can

eliminate. It is, however, a behaviour we need to channel. To do this, first make sure your Bulldog has a number of safe toys to chew. If he has appropriate toys but still prefers to wreak havoc on furniture, then he must be crated.

Much destructive chewing has nothing to do with the normal need to chew. It's a result of boredom or despair. In these cases, the way to stop chewing is to put an end to your dog's boredom. If your Bulldog gets a sufficient amount of exercise and attention, most of his chewing problems will cease.

Food Stealing

Bulldogs are quite attracted to food. After all, it's only natural, and like all mammals they are programmed to be hungry at all times. Dogs do not have an evolved moral sense that tells them stealing is wrong. They are opportunists! The first step in putting a stop to this behaviour is to manage the situation yourself. Don't leave food around if you can help it. Very few dogs have the self-control not to eat a biscuit when it is dropped right in front of them. Controlling this behaviour is more a matter of training yourself to keep your food where it belongs than training the dog.

Noise Phobia

A phobia is defined as an excessive, irrational fear response. Dogs can have them, just as people do, and they can occur in any breed at any age. However, a phobia generally manifests itself first in dogs between the ages of six months and a year. Phobias tend to become more severe as dogs age.

Sometimes a phobia will develop gradually over time, while other times it can emerge after one single scary encounter. Unfortunately, without intervention, the dog may become more afraid with each exposure to the provocation. The phobia can spread to other things as well. A dog may begin by being afraid of thunder, but his phobia may take over to the point where he fears accompanying rain, too, and eventually becomes afraid of rain, even when there is no thunder at all. Whatever the trigger, there seems to be a genetic basis for it.

Noise-phobic dogs may salivate, hide, pace, whine, or pant. Some can even injure themselves in their attempt to escape. They may hide in the bathroom or another cool, dark room. Interestingly enough, dogs prefer humid rooms to hide in, and some people

Thunder Phobia

About 19 percent of dogs have thunder phobia. Dogs may be clued in to approaching thunder by the change in barometric pressure. Dogs appear very sensitive to this, and many appear to find it disturbing. Some dogs simply elect to tear the house apart. Although phobic dogs do tend to hide during a thunderstorm, it doesn't do any good to attempt to lock them up in a crate. This will just increase their anxiety.

suspect that this has to do with the static electricity associated with thunderstorms.

While even the most intelligent dog may fear thunder and fireworks, he may not be able to avoid either of them. In mild cases, you can simply turn on the radio or television—anything to supply a kind of white noise to cover the offending sound.

More serious cases may require sterner measures. While various kinds of psychoactive drugs have been tried on noise-phobic dogs, current research suggests that the best approach to curing your dog of this fear is a two-pronged approach that includes audio recording desensitisation and dog-appeasing pheromones (DAPs). Another solution is melatonin. This natural, over-the-counter hormone is produced by the pineal gland and has a remarkable effect on the thunderstruck. You can buy melatonin in health food stores. Other veterinarians have reported success with a combination of clomipramine and alprazolam. However, you must discuss these options with your veterinarian. What doesn't work is coddling your Bulldog and telling him not to worry. Your very tone will convince him that he has reason to be concerned.

Separation Anxiety

One of the most serious psychological disorders of the contemporary dog is separation anxiety. Technically, it's not even a disorder; it's simply a dog's way of solving a terrible dilemma, like being alone, scared, or bored.

Dogs have been bred and conditioned for millennia to thrive on human company. When that company is missing, some dogs find the pain of separation intolerable. Our canine companions just weren't designed to spend hour after hour alone. Dogs who have suffered abandonment in the past are especially prone to separation anxiety. They have no way of knowing if or when you'll return after you shut that door. This has to be a frightening experience.

People who have dogs who suffer from separation anxiety return home to find shredded sofas, chomped up chairs, ravaged rugs, and a shaking, cowering, or manic dog. And once it starts, it tends to get worse, partly because the owner begins to regard the impending separation with equal fear, although for different reasons—the dread of what she will find when returning home! The dog picks up the owner's tension, and he in turn becomes even more stressed, leading to more destruction, defecation, and despair.

Play Biting

Small puppies can gently mouth your hand without a problem, but by the time the dog is 12 to 16 weeks old, he can be rough. Discourage him from getting carried away. If he bites your hand in play too hard, yip fearfully and leave him to his own devices. He'll soon learn that hard nipping results in the loss of a playmate.

If he starts chewing on an inappropriate object, immediately trade with him for something better and praise him when he actually plays with it or chews it.

Treatment for this serious problem includes a course of therapy that combines careful counterconditioning with appropriate medication. For best results, both should be used together. The behavioural aspect of the therapy is the most difficult, and it should only be undertaken with the help of a certified animal behaviourist, preferably one who is also a veterinarian and can prescribe the medication in appropriate doses

To keep both your home and your Bulldog safe, you may need to confine a destructive dog in your absence. Don't use a crate if you'll be gone long, however. A crated dog simply doesn't have enough to do, and the barrier stress could really bother him. Instead, put him in a large room with a rotating variety of chew toys, a comfortable, inviting bed, and access to water.

To accustom your dog to your absences, practise taking short (just a minute or so) trips at first. Practise getting ready to leave (jingling keys, putting on your coat, even jiggling the door), but don't actually leave. The dog has associated your jingling keys, the act of putting on your coat, and jiggling the door with you leaving. Try dissociating these activities with leaving, and your actual departure may be less stressful for him. In other words, try to defuse the situation by not providing the dog with the accustomed cues you have been giving him as you exit the house.

When you do leave, just go. Don't hang around the house wringing your hands or attempting to comfort the dog with kisses. He'll just feel worse when you finally withdraw. The more you're able to ignore him in the minutes before you leave, the easier the separation will be on him. While you're gone, provide him with a distracting toy, a special something he gets only when you leave. Most dogs enjoy something that contains food. Many items are on the market that have places to stash a few treats, and your dog can spend quite a while figuring out how to remove them. This displaces his anxiety and he may feel much better all day. Leave the television or radio on also. It's comforting to many dogs.

Establishing yourself as a trusted leader is very helpful for dogs with separation anxiety. As the bond between you strengthens, the dog will begin to have faith that you are making the right decisions. If you abdicate your leadership role, your Bulldog will think that he's in charge, and he doesn't really know how to do that. This will lead to more anxiety and more destruction. Be the leader you were born to be and your dog can relax.

In serious cases, you may need to resort to a trained behaviourist and a medical solution.

MEDICATION

As mentioned earlier, when dealing with serious problem behaviours, medication in conjunction with behaviour modification may be the best solution.

Veterinary behaviourists use many of the same kinds of drugs with dogs as physicians use with people. That's because dogs suffer the same types of problems, including phobias, aggression, anxiety, compulsive disorders, hyperactivity, and even self-mutilation. Most psychoactive drugs act by regulating neurotransmitters like serotonin, dopamine, and norepinephrine, which act between the junctions of brain cells. Psychoactive drugs, called Selective Serotonin Reuptake Inhibitors (SSRIs), increase the amount of serotonin available, which tends to stabilise mood and decrease owner-directed aggression. Other drugs can help with separation anxiety, while still others work wonders for senior dogs with canine cognitive dysfunction. However, most of these drugs are not meant to be used alone, but in combination with behavioural training and therapy. Recently, behaviourists have had success with pheromones, particularly DAPs (dog-appeasing pheromones) that have a reassuring effect on dogs. They have no side effects, either, which is a great first step.

To help a Bulldog with separation anxiety, give him a variety of chew toys to play with in your absence.

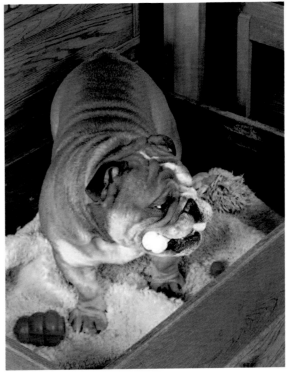

No one training method or medication is a surefire "magic bullet" for all dogs. Every dog is a complex individual who responds differently to a variety of stimuli, just like people. Don't be afraid to experiment with different approaches to get the result you want: a controllable, happy, responsive pet. Your Bulldog is depending on you to make that happen.

ADVANCED TRAINING
and ACTIVITIES
with Your Bulldog

Bulldogs are eligible to participate in many activities, but because of their peculiar anatomy, not to mention interesting character, not all are equally feasible. You know your Bulldog best, but if lure coursing or sheep herding is your dream, your Bulldog can turn it into a nightmare. Fortunately, the Bulldog is one of the world's best companion dogs, and no one need ask for more. At the same time, there are a few things your Bulldog might be interested in, and you should certainly try them out!

Your Bulldog should already know how to sit, lie down, and stay at this point, so what's next? If you're ambitious, all kinds of activities await you and Bulldog. However, before you jump into a new activity, there are a few things you need to keep in mind:

- Research the activity. Figure out if you have the time, money, energy, or even a real interest in whatever activity you're considering.
- Make sure your Bulldog undergoes a thorough veterinary checkup. You not only don't want to work a sick dog, but you want to know what your Bulldog's general health is before you embark on an exercise programme.
- Start slowly. Even if your Bulldog gets a clean bill of health, go slow, just as a human athlete would. Don't stress your dog beyond his natural limits.
- If your dog will be doing endurance work, beef up his fat and protein intake.
- Quit when you've had enough. Remember, you are both supposed to be having *fun*!

GOOD CITIZEN DOG SCHEME

This is a scheme run by the Kennel Club that is designed to reward dogs who have good manners at home and in the community. The programme stresses responsible pet ownership for owners and basic good manners for dogs.

The scheme was launched in 1992. Since then, over 52,000 dogs have passed the test, which is administered through more than 1,000 training organisations.

Any dog is eligible to take art in the Good Citizen Dog Scheme, which is a noncompetitive plan that trains owners and dogs for everyday situations. There are four awards - bronze, silver, gold and puppy foundation assessment - which are based on the level of training that both dog and owner have reached together.

For more information, contact the Kennel Club at www.the-kennel-club.org.uk. This is a great opportunity to develop the bond between dog and owner. You'll both benefit.

Earning a Good Citizen award isn't hard, but it does take preparation and training. Training for the awards is training for good manners and responsible behaviour as well as basic skills evey performance dog should know.

Good Citizen awards are designed to measure just how well-behaved and well-mannered your dog is. You will need a regular buckle collar and lead for the test, but you may not use head halters, harnesses, pinch collars or any other kind of collars or leads. Most of the exercises are performed with your Bulldog on the lead. You will also need your dog's regular brush or comb. You

A show dog must be taught how to stack and stand still while being examined.

The Kennel Club's Good Citizen Dog Scheme

In 1992, the Kennel Club launched a new training programme called the Good Citizen Dog Scheme to promote responsible dog ownership in the UK. Since then, over 52,000 dogs have passed the test, which is administered through 1,050 training organizations.

Any dog is eligible to take part in the Good Citizen Dog Scheme, a noncompetitive plan that trains owners and dogs for everyday situations and grants four awards—bronze, silver, gold, and puppy foundation assessment—based on the level of training that both dog and owner have reached together.

For more information, refer to the Kennel Club's website at www.the-kennel-club.org.uk.

may not use any treats or toys as incentive during the test.

If you dog doesn't pass a test, he can take it again on another occasion. A dog will not pass a test if he doesn't complete any of the exercises, or if he growls, snaps, lunges or bites at the tester or anyone else who is helping in the test.

The exercises become progressively more difficult as you work through bronze, silver and gold levels. The preliminary exercises are very straightforward and include the following:

1. Accepting a friendly stranger
2. Sitting politely for petting
3. Appearance and grooming
4. Out for a walk (walking on a loose lead)
5. Walking through a crowd
6. Sit and down on command and staying in a place
7. Coming when called
8. Reaction to another dog
9. Reaction to distraction
10. Supervised separation

If you think your Bulldog could pass these steps, why not have a go? If not (yet), start training for this test as a goal. Practise each step until your Bulldog is comfortable doing them all. It feels great to earn a Good Citizen award, and you can take pride in knowing that you have a canine good citizen as part of your family.

Local dog shows allow dogs to earn points toward their championship.

DOG SHOWS (CONFORMATION)

Dog Shows in the United Kingdom

Everybody thinks their Bulldogs are beautiful, and many pet owners entertain the thought of trotting their Bulldogs around a dog show ring. But does your Bulldog really have what it takes to compete in the show ring?

Subjective visions of Bulldog beauty aren't relevant when it comes to the conformation ring. While people often liken dog shows to beauty contests, the whole purpose of a dog show is to evaluate breeding stock. While you might find fun matches with less strict rules, the dog show in its classic form judges unneutered and unspayed dogs according to how closely they match the written breed standard - a description of the ideal for any given breed. A neutered pet won't qualify. Breed standards specifically evaluate breeding stock according to that dog's ability to perform the function for which he was originally intended. For Bulldogs, that means they must be built properly and healthy and strong enough to bring down a bull. Although this practice no longer happens, this was the reason that the Bulldog was developed and the reason he is what he is today.

For Kennel Club-sanctioned shows, dogs must be registered with the KC, be six months of age or older, and be a breed recognised in that particular show. Some shows are all-breed shows, which have different judging rings throughout the day or weekend to judge all recognised breeds. Some are group shows. In the case of the Bulldog, these would be Utility dog shows that recognise Poodles, Japanese Shiba Inus, Tibetan Terriers, Dalmations and other dogs which were bred for a specific function and are not included in the sporting and working categories.

Dogs who are competitive in dog shows must closely meet the official written breed standard. Judges study the Bulldog standard and use it to judge Bulldogs according to which one most closely fits the written description of Bulldog perfection. Judges penalise deviations from the breed standard according to their severity. They pet and feel the dog to be sure he is built correctly. They examine the head shape and set of the ears, the eye and muzzle shape, the set of the tail, the shape of the feet, the shape of the body, the condition and quality of the coat, the colour and the way the Bulldog moves. And of course, any Bulldog who appears shy or aggressive or uncooperative will not be winning any prizes.

Your Bulldog might well be the best pet you ever had, and in your eyes flawless. If you aren't breeding your Bulldog, faults don't matter. But if your Bulldog does closely match the breed standard, if you have officially registered your Bulldog with the Kennel Club (or another organisation that sanctions dog shows like the American Kennel Club or the United Kennel Club), and if your dog is not spayed or castrated, you could show your dog in dog shows.

Showing your dog is a lot of fun, not only because it is a great activity to do with your dog, but because you get to spend time seeing a lot of other beautiful dogs, and learning about what exactly makes dogs "correct" according to their breed standards. Some dogs thrive on the attention of the crowd and really ham it up. The best dogs win the title of Champion, and this title is then listed before the dog's name such as Ch. Merriweather's Thunderous Applause (even if you call him Thunder).

How Dog Shows Work

Dog shows can seem pretty complicated when you first attend one and try to work out what is going on, even as a spectator. But this is a highly organised sport. Dogs are trying to earn that coveted title of champion, and to do this, a dog must earn three Challenge Certificates under three different judges. Challenge

What to Wear to Show a Dog

Dog shows are formal events. You won't see jeans and T-shirts out there in the ring. Dogs are supposed to look their best, and so should the handler. However, the handler should not dress to distract from the dog, but to complement the dog.

Conservative is better. Most men wear suits and women wear dresses or jackets and skirts. Choose a colour to best set off your dog's coat.

Certificates are on offer only at Championship shows, and in these competitions the best male and female will be awarded a CC.

In a dog show, dogs are individually exhibited by their handlers. This can be the pet owner, the breeder, or a professonal handler. In the US, professional handlers are used in high-profile dog shows, but in the UK most Bulldogs are handled by their owners. Handlers bring the dogs out into the ring and the judge examines each one, and also watches all the dogs move around the ring together. Typically, the judge eliminates all but a handful at first, then even more carefully studies the finalists.

At the first level, dogs are divided into classes, and in each class, males and females are judged separately. Rosettes will be awarded to dogs in the highest places. When the judge has finished judging all the classes, it is time to find the overall winners.

The judge must look at his class winners and select the best male and the best female. This is no easy task, as he will be evaluating dogs of different ages, from puppies of a mere six months of age, right up to advanced, experienced show dogs. A number of dogs may already be Champions, so it is a very tough challenge for young, upcoming dogs to come forward.

Some Bulldogs enjoy tracking, a sport that involves a harness, long lead, and articles to be tracked, or sniffed out.

The judge will make his choice and will select his winning male and female. If Challenge Certificates are on offer, both dogs will be awarded one. However, there is one final honour the breed judge

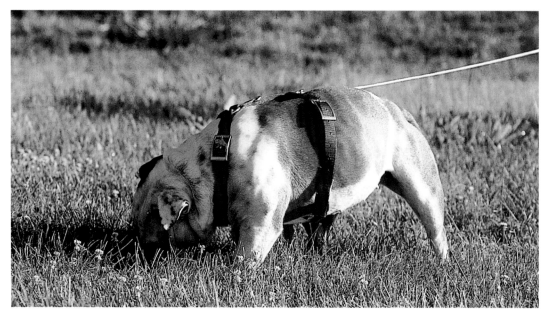

can award - and that is Best of Breed. The judge will make a thorough evaluation of each dog, and will then declare a Best of Breed.

In a breed show, the Best of Breed winner is equivalent to winning Best in Show. But in an all-breed show, the next step is to compete in the Group ring. For Bulldogs, that means competing against such dogs as Poodles, Dalmations and Tibetan Terriers. The best in the Utility group will then go forward to compete against the overall winners of all groups to find the Best in Show. In a large all-breed show this is quite an accomplishment.

What is Agility?

Agility is a competitive sport in which dogs manoeuvre through a timed obstacle course. The course can contain obstacles such as tunnels, jumps, weave poles, and teeter-totters.

OBEDIENCE

Bulldogs are not known as obedience dogs. Although Bulldogs are highly intelligent animals who readily learn basic good manners, most do not shine at formal obedience. One reason for the comparative rarity of their achievements in obedience is that this event requires a dog to retrieve, and Bulldogs are not natural retrievers. They can be taught to go after a ball or stick, but getting them to bring it back is something else again. However, that doesn't mean they can't do it or that they are stupid.

In the UK, you can enter Pre-Beginner, Beginner, Novice, Open, A, B, and Championship C Classes. Exercises include scent discrimination, where your dog is expected to retrieve a particular article from a selection laid out in the ring; distance control, when your dog must obey commands to sit, stand, or down, given while you are standing some distance away from him; and heel work at different speeds and with many different manoeuvres.

AGILITY

Agility is one of the fastest growing canine sports and for good reason. Spend a few minutes watching, and you'll be hooked, too. Although your Bulldog is not likely to make the best time! Most competitive dogs, guided by their handlers, cover such distances in 50 seconds or less. A Bulldog might take 50 days.

Similar to equestrian courses, dogs run as fast as they can while manoeuvring through a timed obstacle course of jumps, tunnels, A-frames, weave poles, ramps and see-saws. While it is possible, many Bulldogs lack the stamina to handle an agility course.

A dog need not be purebred to compete in agility and entrants may also be neutered.

TRACKING

In tracking, your dog will wear a special harness that allows free range of movement. You also need a 20 to 40 foot lead and some "articles," such a wallet or a pair of leather gloves. Both the American Kennel Club and the United Kennel Club offer titles in this sport, although this sport is yet to catch on in the UK.

Bulldogs face the same kinds of difficulties when participating in tracking events that they do in obedience training. They are not natural scent hounds, and although they are quite good at finding things, they prefer to look for them rather than smell the ground. (In that respect, as in so many others, they are like us.) Since tracking dogs are expected to follow a scent on the ground, Bulldogs are at a disadvantage.

EXERCISE AND GAMES

If you have a playful Bulldog, it's a great temptation to get him to run around with you. You have to be careful, though. Not only are the Bulldog's infamous breathing problems a hindrance to vigorous exercise, but too much exercise too early can be detrimental. This is true with many heavy breeds. Until your Bulldog is a year old, walking (not jumping) is the healthiest policy.

For the well-adjusted Bulldog, tug-of-war is a fun game that can be played in a small area.

However, this doesn't mean that you shouldn't give your dog adequate exercise! Bulldogs need it as much as any other dog. While you should give your dog a chance to develop strong bones and ligaments, you need to recognise his limits, even if he does not. The key is to exercise your dog without stressing him.

As a rule, Bulldogs are more like philosophers than athletes. While you may have one who enjoys fetch or tugging on a rope, it's not a given. Experiment with different activities to see what your particular dog enjoys!

Kennel Club Sporting Events

The Kennel Club in the United Kingdom sponsors a variety of events for Bulldogs and their owners to enjoy together. For complete listings, rules, and descriptions, please refer to the Kennel Club's website at www.the-kennel-club.org.uk.

Agility

Introduced in 1978 at Crufts, agility is a fun, fast-paced, and interactive sport. The event mainly consists of multiple obstacles on a timed course that a dog must handle. Different classes have varying levels of difficulty.

Flyball

Flyball is an exciting sport introduced at Crufts in 1990. Competition involves a relay race in which several teams compete against each other and the clock. Equipment includes hurdles, a flyball box, backstop board, and balls.

Obedience

Obedience competitions test owner and dog's ability to work together as a team. There are seven different classes to work your way through - each progressively more difficult.

Walking and Jogging

Don't expect to get a lot of exercise yourself while walking a Bulldog. They don't go very fast (for a dog), and they like to take their time to examine their surroundings. Allow them this pleasure, and take some time to enjoy the surroundings yourself. You can always jog later. At the same time, I can't overemphasise the importance of allowing your Bulldog to move at his own pace. These animals are very susceptible to heatstroke, as I discuss in Chapter 8. If you desire a jogging companion, another breed is a better choice.

Fetch

Bulldogs can fetch, but many would prefer not to. In many

Participating in activities, like fetch, is a great way to exercise your Bulldog.

instances, a Bulldog is quite anxious to get the ball but not particularly interested in giving it back. In that case, the dog has taken charge of the game. To regain control, throw the toy, and when your Bulldog has picked it up, run in the opposite direction. When he gets close enough, take the toy by trading it for a treat. Try this method a few more times.

Some Bulldogs are simply not interested in chasing a ball or toy at all. If this is the case with your dog, try something else, like tug-of-war.

Tug-of-War

For a long time, people were told not to play tug with their dogs, as it made them aggressive and dominant. This is not true, although you probably should avoid this game with an animal who has had domination or aggression problems in the past. For the normal Bulldog, however, tug-of-war is a perfectly suitable game. It provides great exercise and can be played in a small area.

Select a simple tug toy like a tug rope that the dog will come to recognise as the cue for the game, and use it only for tug-of-war. Devise a special command to begin the game, like "Let's TUG!" Your dog will naturally want to grab the tug rope. If he grabs the rope without permission, don't play—he should release it on command. If he does not do this, teach him by trading the rope for a treat. As soon as you get the rope from him, give it right back and praise him. This will make him more amenable to giving up his cherished rope. If he runs off with the toy, don't chase him. He'll soon return with it for more tugs.

You can also interrupt the game with a few obedience commands from time to time. This will sharpen his skills and keep him listening to you. Don't allow the dog to touch you with his teeth. If you receive a nip, stop the game immediately for at least five minutes. He'll get the picture.

THERAPY DOGS

Therapy dogs comfort the sick, cheer the elderly, and heal those who are suffering from emotional issues. They provide benefits for heart patients, AIDS patients, the disabled, and homeless children. They have even been used to help rehabilitate prisoners! Fortunately, the calm, friendly, and charming Bulldog makes the ideal therapy dog. They are sturdy enough not to be easily knocked over and small enough not to be clumsy or intimidating in hospitals and nursing homes. They are also soft and don't mind being petted.

In the UK, an organisation called Pets as Therapy tests dogs for their suitability for therapy work. If your dog is successful you can become an accredited representative. In some cases, you'll just be making the rounds, visiting and talking with residents (many of whom have literally no one else to talk to). In other cases, your pet will be part of a specific treatment plan, with clear goals set forth on each visit.

Certification programmes vary, but many require that your dog complete a full obedience course and a health screening and be of a certain age (usually one year). Of course, a good therapy dog should be bathed and groomed (especially the nails) and flea-free. As far as personality is concerned, two qualities are of the essence: friendliness and obedience. To find out what programmes may be available in your area, contact a local nursing home or hospital or find further information at the Pets as Therapy website - www.petsastherapy.org.

C h a p t e r

8

HEALTH

of Your Bulldog

Nothing is more important than your Bulldog's health. As his owner and guardian, you are largely responsible for maintaining it. The keys to health, which include the proper diet and exercise, preventive care, and clean surroundings, are in your hands!

VISITING THE VETERINARIAN

Your Bulldog's happiness depends largely on his health. To that end, a good relationship with a wise and compassionate veterinarian is essential. Next to you, your vet is your dog's best friend.

It's a good idea to secure a vet before you even bring your Bulldog home. Look for one you can trust who understands the special nature of Bulldogs.

Questions to Ask the Vet

If this is the first trip to the veterinarian for you and your Bulldog, check the place out—don't be afraid to ask for a tour. Also, consider the following questions when making this very important choice for you and your canine companion:

- Do staff members seem relaxed, friendly, and compassionate, or do they have a "this is just a business" aura?
- What services do they provide? Boarding? Grooming? Home visits?
- Are any of the staff specialists in orthopaedics, holistic treatments, behaviour, or cardiology?
    - What hours is the clinic open? Evenings? Weekends? Who answers the calls when the surgery is closed? (If you work days, you should choose a clinic with evening hours.)
    - How close is the vet to your home? A difference of five minutes can mean life or death for your Bulldog.

- Does the clinic accept pet insurance?
- Is the clinic a member of a spay/neuter programme?
- How many Bulldogs does the clinic handle, and how familiar is the staff with the Bulldog's special health concerns?

One of the most important things to remember when researching veterinarians is that you need the help of a vet versed in Bulldogdom. Bulldogs are a peculiar breed with special health problems (especially respiratory), particularly when it comes to anaesthesia. Many otherwise excellent vets are stymied when it comes to this breed. However, once you find a good vet, never let her go!

The First Visit

Because your Bulldog's health is so important, finding a vet you trust is essential.

Make the first visit to the vet a fun one, with lots of treats, pets, and playtime. If all goes well, the first trip will be for a checkup only, so your dog won't have any painful associations with the visit. If you are calm and happy yourself, your mood will definitely rub off on your Bulldog. On the other hand, if you're tense and nervous, you'll convey these feelings to the dog.

Make sure the first checkup takes place within 48 hours of getting your Bulldog, if possible, and bring along a stool sample so the veterinarian can check for worms, most of which are invisible to the naked eye. If he's not a show dog, you should also make a spay/neuter appointment. He'll live a longer, healthier, happier life, and you'll be doing your bit to reduce the problem of pet overpopulation. Of course, you should take your Bulldog to your vet for regular checkups as well.

The initial checkup will include a good look at your dog's teeth, eyes, and ears. Your vet will listen to his heart and lungs to detect heart murmurs, an irregular heartbeat, or harsh lung sounds. There will be a general inspection for lumps and bumps, dry skin, fleas, and ticks. Your Bulldog will also be weighed, and you'll probably receive a lecture on feeding and nutrition. The vet may test each limb and joint for range of motion, and she may poke your dog's stomach to check for pain or enlarged organs. The belly button will be examined for an umbilical hernia.

Owner Responsibilities

Of course, you have a responsibility for your Bulldog's health too! Good Bulldog owners know their part of the equation includes:

- Supplying a good diet
- Providing adequate exercise
- Keeping the dog up-to-date on vaccinations and regular health checkups
- Brushing the dog's teeth daily
- Grooming regularly and using that opportunity to check ears, eyes, teeth, and nails.
- Observing the dog's habits and noting any changes
- Loving, cuddling, and interacting with the dog

Even if your dog appears to be healthy and in top condition, it is important to have a yearly check up by your vet. This can be combined with your annual vaccination trip to the surgery.

VACCINATIONS

Vaccinations save lives. Before the days of effective veterinary vaccines, dogs were victims of canine distemper, hepatitis, and rabies. Now these diseases are rare. When parvo first emerged on the scene in the late 1970s, many dogs died before a vaccine was developed. While there is an ongoing discussion about how often and against what diseases your dog needs to be vaccinated, you owe it to your dog and your community to do your research and make an informed choice. Consult with your veterinarian to ask about his vaccine protocol, and don't be afraid to ask questions.

Vaccination Protocol

While vaccination scheduling is a matter of controversy (and is constantly changing), here are the current recommendations for most dogs.

Questions to Ask the Vet

Many times I get calls from people who say, "My vet diagnosed my dog with Carpiothyburoforkoliosis (or whatever). How bad is that? Should he be on a special diet? Is it catching?"

I always respond, "Well, I don't know. What did your vet say?"

They reply, "I didn't ask." Or, "He told me but I forgot." Or, "He told me but I didn't understand what he meant."

Don't be afraid to ask your veterinarian questions! Ensuring that you are well-informed will assist you in making the best choices for your beloved Bulldog. Here are some of the most important questions to ask if your dog has been diagnosed with a serious ailment:

- **"What does my dog have, exactly?"** Get both the official medical name for the disorder as well as a down-to-earth explanation of what it means.

- **"What's the prognosis?"** This means you're asking your vet to predict the final outcome of the disease. Is the disease curable? Treatable? If not, will it eventually kill your dog? These are hard questions, but you need to know.

- **"What's the best course of action, and how will it help my dog?"** Your vet may want to perform surgery or use radiation, herbs, or acupuncture, so you need to find out what he wants to do and how it will help.

- **"How will this disease and its treatment affect my dog?"** You'll want to know if your dog will be listless, lose his appetite, or experience problems with housetraining. If the disease is transmittable to your other dogs, you will want to know that also.

- **"What responsibility will I have for his care?"** Your dog's illness may require you to medicate him regularly or even take him for treatments elsewhere.

- **"Should my pet see a specialist?"** Veterinary medicine has as many specialists as human medicine does. You are not insulting your general practitioner vet if you ask to see an oncologist, ophthalmologist, or whatever specialist your dog may require.

- **"How much will this cost?"** This is a fair and legitimate question. Ask it.

- **"When should I check back if my dog is not improving as expected?"** You should be aware of the progress your dog is expected to make within a certain time period. This will help you determine when to further consult with your vet.

Finally, get everything in writing, and don't leave the surgery until you completely understand. If you get home and realise you forgot to ask something, call your vet back. If you are not satisfied with something and can't work it out, see a different vet. There's no profit in wandering about in ignorance or uncertainty, and your Bulldog will be the one who suffers.

Puppies 4 to 20 Weeks of Age

The vaccination series begins between six and eight weeks of age. Typically, the last vaccination is given between 14 and 16 weeks of age. These early vaccines should protect against canine distemper virus, leptospirosis, parainfluenza, infectious canine hepatitis and canine parvovirus. In cases where your dog is exposed to others in a closed area, a vaccine against bordetella is recommended.

Dogs 20 Weeks to 2 Years of Age

Young adults need booster shots to ensure lifelong immunity against the same diseases they were vaccinated against as puppies.

Dogs Over 2 Years of Age

If your dog has had his puppy shots and boosters, you and your vet may wish to forgo further vaccination for three or four years. It is increasingly recognised that annual vaccinations are not necessary, although annual checkups certainly are!

Diseases to Protect Against

Although vaccination protocols differ from place to place and even from vet to vet, consider vaccinating your puppy against the following diseases.

Parvovirus

Parvovirus is a highly contagious, deadly virus that first appeared in 1978. It is transmitted through the faeces of infected dogs. This virus invades and destroys rapidly growing cells in the intestine, bone marrow, lymphoid tissue, and even the heart muscles, resulting in nausea, depression, vomiting, and severe bloody diarrhoea. The disease can vary from mild to fatal, especially in puppies if they are not properly treated. To make matters worse, parvo is a cold-hardy virus, which means that it can survive in infected faeces at temperatures as low as 4°F (-15°C). The incubation period is from two to seven days.

Young adults need booster shots to protect them from various diseases.

Distemper

Distemper is the main killer of dogs worldwide. It destroys the nervous system and attacks every tissue in the body. It is caused by an airborne, measles-like virus. The incubation period is 7 to 21 days, and initial symptoms include lethargy, fever, runny nose, and yellow discharge from the eyes. The dog will demonstrate laboured breathing, lose his appetite, and experience diarrhoea and vomiting. Later symptoms include a nervous twitch, seizures, and thickening of the paw pads and nose, which is why the disease was once known as "hardpad." Dogs who progress to this stage are unlikely to make a complete recovery.

Hepatitis

Hepatitis is a serious disease caused by an adenovirus and is most dangerous in puppies. It is spread by contact with an infected dog or the infected dog's urine or faeces. The white blood cell count drops, and some dogs experience clotting problems. It also affects the kidneys and liver. Symptoms include high fever, red mucous membranes, depression, and loss of appetite. Small blood spots may appear on the gums, and the eyes will look bluish. Even dogs who recover often experience chronic illnesses; they may also shed the virus for months, infecting others in the process. Luckily, this disease is seldom seen nowadays, largely because of the effective vaccines against it.

Leptospirosis

Leptospirosis is a worldwide bacterial infection that can be passed on to human beings. Dogs can contract this disease through exposure to the urine of an infected dog, rat, or wild animal. Leptospirosis affects the liver and kidneys, and in its most dangerous form can even shut the kidneys down. Even if the dog survives the disease, he can have permanent kidney damage. Treatment includes s, and in the case of kidney failure, dialysis. A vaccine is available for some forms of leptospirosis; however, many vets do not recommend its use, especially for young puppies. The "older" forms of leptospirosis are seldom seen nowadays, and the vaccine can cause reactions in some dogs. Recently, the disease has returned in a new and virulent strain, one that was previously seen only in horses and cows. A vaccine against this "new" lepto strain is being tested.

If you are not sure which vaccinations are needed for your dog and your circumstances, ask your vet for her recommendations.

Rabies

This is not applicable to dogs born in the UK, but it is important if you plan to take your dog overseas. Rabies is a fatal virus that attacks the nervous system and causes encephalitis. Rabies is transmitted in saliva from infected animals. Symptoms include personality changes, fever, aggression, salivation, paralysis and death.

Bordetella

Bordetella is also known as "kennel cough." This is important if your dog will be visiting a lot of other dogs or if he is going to be housed in a kennel. Many organisms can cause this condition, which is like a bad cold in older dogs but more serious in puppies. True to its name, dogs with bordetella cough, wheeze, hack, and sneeze. It can spread very rapidly through a kennel because the virus is airborne. The vaccine commonly given for kennel cough needs to be administered every six months to be effective, although it does not protect against all forms of the disease. No cure exists—only supportive treatment, and in some cases, antibiotics.

Bordetella Immunisation

Immunisation against Bordetella is recommended annually for any dog who is frequently around other dogs, such as in a kennel or at a dog show.

Coronavirus

Coronavirus is a disease related to the human cold. Most serious in puppies, coronavirus is passed through food that has been contaminated by the faeces of an infected dog. It can also be picked up from any contaminated surface that a dog may lick. It is very contagious and produces vomiting, diarrhoea, and depression, symptoms similar to those of parvovirus. The stool of the dog will also be yellowish. Fortunately, this disease is not quite as severe as parvovirus, but there is no real cure—only supportive care.

Lyme Disease

Lyme disease is rare in the UK, but its incidence is increasing. It can be transmitted if your dog is bitten by a deer tick. Symptoms of this chronic bacterial infection include depressed appetite, weight loss, lethargy, fever and, primarily, lameness and swollen joints. Possible development of arthritis and heart inflammation can occur. Immunisation is available against Lyme Disease, but the efficacy is variable and is recommended only for dogs who live in areas with high tick infestation.

PARASITES

Parasites cause problems that can result in something as simple as mild itching or something much more severe, such as death. External parasites include mites (sarcoptic, demodex, ear, or cheyletiella), fleas, and ticks. Internal parasites usually include worms like roundworm, hookworm, whipworm, and heartworm. Many of these parasites can be prevented or kept under control with preventive medications.

External Parasites

External parasites live on but not inside your dog's body. With the exception of some mites, they are usually visible.

Fleas

Fleas are truly amazing creatures. They can jump 150 times their own length, accelerate faster than a race car, and live for up to a year without eating. A female can lay 2,000 eggs in her lifetime. Despite these charming attributes, many people seem to dislike fleas. This may be because they are bloodsucking and itchy, causing allergic reactions and transmitting tapeworm along the way. They can bite people, too, although they prefer dogs. Strangely, the most common flea found on the dog is the cat flea. Besides constant scratching, a sure sign that your dog has fleas is the presence of blackish/reddish granules. These are flea faeces, and they are largely composed of your dog's blood.

The most effective treatments for most dogs are adulticide spot-ons. The word "adulticide" means the product kills adult fleas. Put a few drops between your Bulldog's shoulder blades just once a month. The product spreads over the skin surface but doesn't enter the bloodstream, making it a safe option for most dogs. A flea that even lands on your dog will die. Some adulticide formulations also kill ticks on contact. Another type of effective product contains an insect growth regulator, or IGR. These keep flea eggs from hatching, so they never grow into adults. These can be topical or come in pill form.

The most popular spot-on adulticides and insect growth regulators are available from your vet, but you can also buy spot on adulticides and insect growth regulators over the counter in pet shops. Some people say they work just as well as the more expensive prescription brands, and other people insist they are not

Vaccinating the Senior Dog

There are basically two camps of opinion regarding vaccinating older animals. Some say that older dogs have a weakened immune system and need more frequent vaccinations. Others maintain that older dogs have built up a sufficient body of immunisations through their regular vaccines, meaning they need fewer (or no) vaccinations. Discuss these options with your vet.

Check your Bulldog for parasites like fleas and ticks after returning indoors.

as effective or safe. Ask your vet for for a recommendation.

Other non-prescription flea treatments like flea collars, sprays, powders and dips may be cheaper but expose your dog to more pesticides, because they must be used more often to be effective, although for mild infestatons, they might work. They also have more side effects.

Some people have had luck with natural alternatives to conventional flea or tick medications. Garlic, for example, has been popular for centuries. Not all natural alternatives are equally effective, however. It's important to consult with your veterinarian before selecting a particular remedy.

Ticks

Superficially, ticks look like insects, but deep down they are arachnids, more akin to spiders than bugs. Although a tick or two doesn't seem to cause any discomfort to the affected dog the way a flea infestation does, all 850 species of tick are extremely dangerous. They carry an almost interminable list of diseases, including Lyme disease, ehrlichiosis, babesiosis, tularaemia, and tick paralysis, depending on where you live.

Ticks can transmit diseases to your Bulldog and also to you.

These tiny arachnids swell to many times their normal size when filled with a blood meal. Lyme disease is one of the most common tick-borne illnesses that can affect both dogs and humans. It is still rare in the UK, but its incidence is increasing. Lyme disease can cause swollen joints and painful arthritis, and serious cases can cause serious heart and kidney damage. If ticks are a problem in your area, consider using an adulticide spot-on that also kills ticks. Also, after time in tick-prone areas, go over your Bulldog carefully with a flea comb. If you find a tick, you can remove it manually, but don't use your bare hands. If the swollen tick bursts and you get the blood on your hands, the bacteria can actually infect you through your skin.

Mites

Mites are arachnids that are related to spiders. Altogether there are over 30,000 kinds of mites, but only a dozen or so infect dogs. The following are some problems your dog may encounter if infested with mites.

Tick Removal

To remove a tick, first douse it with alcohol. Then, wearing rubber gloves or using tweezers or special tick remover, pull the tick straight back away from the bite. Don't pull straight up or the head may break off and remain under the skin. Flush the tick immediately, or drop into a cup of alcohol until you can dispose of it.

• **Ear mites.** Ear mites are very small, crab-like creatures that live in the ear canals. They cause a foul odour in the ear and cause the dog to shake his head. Because these symptoms can be caused by a wide variety of problems, it is best to have the ears examined by a vet before instilling medication that can make an accurate diagnosis more difficult. Several medications are available to treat ear mites, and your veterinarian will advise what is best for your dog.

• **Demodectic mange.** Demodectic mange, also called red mange, is a fairly common skin disease that most generally affects puppies. While the culprit, Demodex canis, can be found on most dogs, only some seem to suffer adverse effects, probably due to a defective immune system. There is also a hereditary component.

When the disease is present, mites crowd out the hair follicles, causing the hair to fall out. In addition, the follicles often become infected and the skin becomes red and inflamed. A skin scraping can be made to confirm the diagnosis. Mange in puppies usually resolves itself, but it can also be treated with insecticides. If an adult dog contracts demodectic mange, it's a sign that the immune system may be compromised. Adult-onset demodectic mange is very serious and requires almost continual attention. The outcome is far from assured, however.

• **Sarcoptic mange (scabies).** This is a highly contagious parasitic disease affecting both humans and dogs. The culprit is a microscopic mite called Sarcoptes scabiei. The mites burrow in the skin and cause itchiness, redness, and hair loss in both people and dogs. (This mite can affect almost any kind of animal, by the way, especially livestock.) Sarcoptic mange is treated with special shampoos, dips, pills, or injections.

Internal Parasites

Some troubling parasites, like worms and giardia, make their living inside your dog—completely invisible even to the most observant owner. The only way you will discover your dog has them is by learning how they can physically affect your pet.

Internal parasites can afflict both puppies and adult dogs, as well as people. There are dozens of varieties, and different species can infect different parts of the dog's body. A few kinds attack the oesophagus and stomach, but the most common ones go for the small intestine (like roundworms, hookworms, threadworms, trichina worms, tapeworms, and flukes). Still other parasites, like whipworms, target the caecum and colon. In fact, almost every organ of the dog's body, including the liver, nasal cavity, trachea, lungs, heart, kidneys, nervous system, arteries, and veins, can be prey to one kind of worm or another.

Some worms are transmitted though food. Freezing meat to 40°F (-40°C) for two days or heating it to 140°F (60°C) kills them. Of course, finding a place to freeze anything at -40°F (-40°C) is a bit of a problem unless you live in a laboratory.

The only way to keep your dog worm-free is to use a regular dewormer on your dog and keep his quarters and your garden clean and picked up. When you bring your puppy to the vet for his first checkup, she should ask you to bring a stool sample, which she will inspect for internal parasites. Your vet can then periodically check your dog for evidence of parasites, and if necessary, prescribe medication to get rid of them.

Giardia (*Giardia lamblia*)

Giardia Vaccination is not recommended by most vets, because it does not prevent infection. The internal parasite that causes giardiasis can be passed from pets to people but most human cases of giardiasis come from human sources, not dogs. *Giardia* is a

Flea Fact

Fleas, if swallowed, can cause tapeworm infestation. Long-term flea infestation can result in anaemia, which can be serious, even deadly, in small puppies.

parasite that dogs can pick up from an affected water source, such as puddles at parks or untested well water.

Roundworm (*Toxocara canis*)

This is the most common worm of all. Nearly all puppies are born with roundworms, which they acquire from their mother. Roundworms penetrate the small intestine and can be carried through the bloodstream to the liver, lungs, and even up the trachea, where they are swallowed. At this point in time, the worms begin their life cycle all over again, producing eggs that are excreted with the faeces. The worms can move to muscle tissue, where they form cysts and go dormant. Older dogs are less likely to be infected, but they can pick them up from contaminated soil.

Hookworm (*Ancylostoma caninum*)

Hookworms attach to the intestinal wall with their teeth and cause intestinal bleeding. The larvae are deposited in faeces, where they can be easily picked up again, either through the skin or by mouth. They like shady, sandy areas best, so barefoot children are especially at risk. Remember, hookworms don't have to be swallowed; the larvae can actually penetrate the skin and cause lesions. Dogs infected by hookworms can develop chronic intestinal bleeding and consequent pain and anaemia. Because the worms absorb nutrients, they can also cause malnutrition.

Whipworm (*Trichuris vulpis*)

Whipworms are one of the most difficult of all worms to destroy. Their eggs seem impervious to time and cold weather, and a female whipworm can lay 2,000 eggs a day. Those aren't good statistics. Severe infestations can give a dog a terrible case of colitis, and they can even be fatal.

Tapeworm (*Dipylidium caninum*)

Tapeworm eggs may be found in faeces or around your dog's anal opening. Tapeworm is spread by fleas. Although not as serious in dogs as in people, tapeworm requires a special dewormer to get rid of it. Dogs may not have overt signs of tapeworms other than the telltale eggs in the faeces, but they should be eliminated as soon as possible because they compete for nutrients. They can also migrate into the bile duct, causing liver problems. Often, however,

Pyrethrins

Pyrethrins have been used to kill insects for over 100 years. They are made from the extracts of chrysanthemums and have a wide safety margin. A synthetic compound similar to pyrethrins is permethrin. It lasts a lot longer than pyrethrins but cannot be used on cats.

tapeworms seem to live rather amicably inside the dog.

Another common species, *Taenia pisiformis,* can be picked up by ingesting infected rabbits and rodents.

Ringworm (*Microsporum canis*)

Despite its name, ringworm is a fungus, and a highly contagious one at that. Dogs can pick it up from an infected dog or even from the ground. It is more common in puppies than in adult dogs. Classical signs include scabs or an irregularly shaped area of skin infection (not always a ring). There may be rapid hair loss at the site. People, especially children, can get ringworm from dogs, so get it treated immediately.

To avoid worms, keep your garden clean.

The specific treatment for your dog will depend on the severity of the infection, how many pets are involved, if there are children in the household, and how difficult it will be to disinfect your dog's environment. The most common treatment is griseofulvin, an oral medication.

Heartworm (*Dirofilaria immitis*)

These worms are rarely found in the UK, but are present in most of the United States. Heartworms are big creatures related to roundworms that live in the right side and large blood vessels of the heart, causing them to become obstructed. Badly infected dogs can have hundreds of these worms residing in their hearts, and they can live there for years. They lay very tiny larvae called microfilariae that can live up to three years in the bloodstream. When they reproduce, their offspring, in the form of microfilariae, circulate in the bloodstream where they can be sucked up by mosquitoes, where they then develop further. Later, they migrate to the mosquito's mouth and enter a new host.

The roundworm, this helminth lives in contaminated soil or faeces, and the larvae sometimes enter the body throuhg the skin. If signs are noticeable, they include watery diarrhoea and symptoms of lung infection.

It takes six to seven months between the time when an animal was bitten until the adult heartworms develop. Signs of infection include coughing, fluid accumulation, decreased appetite, and heart failure. Various tests are used to detect infection. When left untreated, this disease is nearly always fatal.

Treatment for heartworm is risky, long, and difficult, but it is better than dying from the disease. The treatment itself is a two-step process, as the adult worms and the microfilaria must be killed separately. (No one medication kills both.) The adults are treated first, and then a different treatment is used to kill the microfilaria and migrating larvae. As the worms die, they lodge in the lung arteries and block even more blood vessels than before treatment. The inflammation is then amplified because of the decomposing worms inside the blood vessels. Powerful medication will rid your dog of the heartworm, but it is a treatment with risks. (This is why the best "cure" for heartworm is prevention of the disease in the first place.) If you are travelling overseas your vet can prescribe a preventive medication that will keep your precious Bulldog free of heartworm. Any dog can get heartworm from even one mosquito bite, so take the safe path and keep your dog on medication. The medication will kill immature heartworms but can't be used to kill adult worms. It works by immediately killing any heartworm larvae acquired within the previous 30 days. Heartworm medication also prevents your dog from acquiring hookworms, roundworms, and whipworms.

COMMON DISEASES

In this section, we'll look at several common diseases of dogs, arranged according to the system that the disease affects.

Cancer

Cancer isn't really one disease. It's a general term for more than 200 different types of malignancies that can affect any part of the body. All cancers, however, work basically the same way: They result from too rapid cell growth—the cells are all "undifferentiated," meaning that they can no longer be recognised as a liver cell, skin cell, or whatever kind of cell they were supposed to be. Cancer cells also have apparently developed something like an "immortality gene," and so unlike normal cells that are born and die, cancer cells just go on indefinitely.

New treatments for cancer are on the horizon. One promising new route that is still in its experimental stage is brachytherapy. In this procedure, doctors introduce radiation-emitting beads directly into the tumour site using a hollow tube. This operation lets the doctor target the cancer directly without affecting other tissues. It is important to realise that no one cancer treatment is right for every dog. Age and even personality type may dictate the best kind of treatment. Costs can also vary widely, ranging from little more than average surgery or medication costs to several thousand pounds.

Heartworm Prevention

Heartworms are rare in the UK, but if you are travelling abroad with your Bulldog check with your veterinarian regarding preventatives before you go.

Eye Disorders

People used to believe that dogs could see in black and white only. We now know that dogs can see colour, although not exactly the way people do. Dogs can see various shades of blue and can even distinguish among different shades of grey that people see as one colour. However, dogs cannot distinguish between red, yellow, orange, and green, which is pretty simple for most of us.

Unfortunately, dogs can contract various different types of eye disorders, including many of the same ones that affect people, like cataracts and glaucoma. The most common ones are listed here.

Irritation

To relieve eye irritation due to smoke, dust, wind, or pollen, rinse the eyes with a clear solution made for ophthalmic use. You can even use contact lens drops.

Cherry Eye (Eversion of the Nictitating Membrane)

This common problem in Bulldogs is due to the extrusion of a gland that normally stays under the lower eyelid at the inside corner of the eye. It appears as a round, red mass. It looks terrible and should be surgically restored to its normal position. (The gland should not be removed, however, as doing so will result in "dry eye," a painful and serious condition.)

SARD

SARD is the acronym for Sudden Acquired Retinal Degeneration. It is indeed sudden, often literally striking overnight and blinding your dog, although in some cases it takes a week or even two to develop. Other senses may also be dulled. The condition is painless and may be accompanied by weight gain, increased appetite, and thirst. Any breed can be affected, and most victims are females between the ages of 7 and 14. The cause is unknown, but stress, lawn pesticides, and autoimmune disease may all be implicated. There is no cure or treatment for this disease at the present time.

Entropion

In this condition, which is common in Bulldogs, the lower (usually) eyelid rolls inward and brings the lashes into direct contact with the cornea. It is very irritating to the eye. Many dogs are born with entropion, but it can also be acquired later in life as a result of corneal eye disease or other causes. One or both eyes may be affected. Signs of entropion include tearing, squinting, rubbing, discharge, and rolling of the eyelid. Surgical treatment is the only cure, but it needs to be done by a veterinarian experienced in the procedure. (Overcorrection leads to other problems.) After surgery, your Bulldog will probably wear a special collar to prevent him from reinjuring the eye. Sometimes antibiotics will be prescribed as well. Because this is an inherited condition, affected animals should not be bred.

Glaucoma

Glaucoma is a painful condition that occurs when pressure inside the eyeball increases to dangerous levels. This is the most common cause of blindness in dogs and cats. It occurs when the small drainage sties within the eyeball are narrowed or blocked. The result is usually permanent damage to the retina, causing severe pain and blindness. Often the cause is heritable, but the disease can also result from injury, tumours, or infections.

Glaucoma is a veterinary emergency that requires immediate attention to have any chance of saving the eye. Signs include squinting, drainage, and sometimes swelling of the eye. Diagnosis is based on pressure measurement of the eyes, although other tests may be used to find underlying causes. Blood

Common Signs

There are some common signs of cancer in small animals (and notice how similar these signs are to cancer in human beings):

- Abnormal swellings that persist or continue to grow
- Sores that don't heal
- Weight loss
- Loss of appetite
- Bleeding or discharge from any body opening
- Offensive odour
- Difficulty eating or swallowing
- Hesitation to exercise or loss of stamina
- Persistent lameness or stiffness
- Difficulty breathing, urinating, or defecating

work, an ultrasound, and CAT scans may also be used to determine underlying causes. If blindness results, the eye may be injected with an agent that removes the pressure; however, the dog will remain blind. Sometimes a severely damaged eye must be surgically removed. The goal of both procedures is to relieve pain.

Blindness

Any number of conditions can produce blindness, including glaucoma, retinal disease, trauma, cataracts, and corneal problems. While it's certainly no fun, blindness is not the tragedy for dogs that it is for many humans. Most dogs make a remarkable adjustment, and their owners are usually more traumatised than the dogs. Some owners make the mistake of carrying their dogs around. Don't do this; let your Bulldog learn to navigate on his own—it'll be an adventure for him. Use a lead to take him to new places.

While dogs do depend on their eyes, they have keen ears and a good nose to considerably make up for their loss of sight. Dogs who lose their vision suddenly have more problems than others, but even these dogs eventually come around and return to a

Your vet can check for common eye ailments at your Bulldog's annual physical exam.

normal doggy life. Some dogs who go blind slowly adapt so well that their owners are unaware of the fact that darkness has finally fallen. These owners may not figure it out until they change the furniture around.

To help your dog adjust, maintain as much stability in the home as possible. Keep furniture shifting to a minimum, and if you do have to move it, take the dog around so he learns the new arrangement. Even leaving a relatively small thing in an unaccustomed place may cause some confusion. Protect your dog by removing dangerous objects and covering areas of water that he might tumble into. Put a "blind dog" tag on his collar so that if he becomes lost, the finder will have a clue as to his condition.

Some dogs learn to navigate by holding a buffering object like a stuffed toy as they move from place to place. You can even purchase a special device that fits around the dog and protects him. Most dogs learn to navigate their own environments so well that they don't need this, however.

Because a blind dog can't see you, it's wise to speak before touching him (and shocking the heck out of him). Feed him at the same time in the same place every day and supervise his outdoor activity.

Ear Infections

Signs of an ear infection include pawing at the ears, as well as tilting or shaking the head. The ears themselves will probably give off a foul odour. For most cases of ear infection, your vet will prescribe a medication that can be applied to the ear. (Some infections are bacterial, some are fungal, and some are a mixture of both, so using the correct medication is important.)

For dogs with chronic infections, the vet may want to flush the ear out under anaesthesia. It is too painful to be done well when the animal is awake. Afterward, you'll need to clean and treat the ear daily. If the infection subsides, the ear must still be cleaned for the rest of the dog's life.

Allergies

Like people, dogs suffer from various allergies. In most cases, allergic reactions are annoying but not life-threatening. Your dog doesn't usually sneeze when he has an allergy, however. Sometimes allergies express themselves as urticaria (hives) or angioedema. Urticaria is a condition characterised by small bumps in the skin and is a typical hypersensitive or allergic reaction. Sometimes the bumps are itchy, but not always. A related condition is angioedema, or swelling of the face, especially around the muzzle and eyes. These reactions typically develop within 20 minutes of exposure to the allergen. They aren't usually life-threatening, although severe swelling around the throat can make breathing even more difficult for a Bulldog. The treatment is generally antihistamines, but if breathing is affected, epinephrine is administered.

Allergies

The most common allergies affecting dogs are:
- Atopic dermatitis
- Contact allergy
- Flea allergy
- Food allergy
- Hot spots
- Insect stings

One of the most severe allergic reactions is anaphylaxis, a life-threatening condition that may include shock, respiratory and cardiac failure, and death. Anything that can cause an allergic reaction can cause anaphylaxis, including insect stings, antibiotics, vaccines or other medications, and even foods. It is rare but deadly. Common signs include sudden diarrhoea, vomiting, pale gums, fast heart rate, shock, seizures, coma, and death. Unlike many other kinds of allergic reactions, there is no facial swelling. This is an extreme emergency—your dog needs epinephrine right away. Immediately drive to the nearest vet clinic. Intravenous fluids, oxygen, and other medications may also be needed. While it is not known exactly what may cause animals to react so badly, dogs who have previously had an allergic reaction (like hives) are most at risk. If your dog suffers severe allergic reactions that affect his breathing, you may be able to secure an "epi-pen" from your vet, a syringe and needle containing a single dose of epinephrine for future emergencies.

There's no real cure for allergies, but several treatment options are available, ranging from avoiding the allergen (not easy), to administering special shampoos and oils, to dispensing medications. Check with your vet to determine the best option for you and your Bulldog.

The following are some of the most common allergies affecting dogs.

Atopic Dermatitis

Atopic dermatitis (AD) is a very common skin condition in dogs caused by airborne allergens like dust mites, mould, or pollen. While some dogs seem to be able to tolerate a lot of that stuff, others can't—just like people. The first clinical signs of AD appear when the dog is between six months and three years of age.

In the beginning, you will likely notice that your dog seems to be itchy; he may rub his face or lick his feet. Then, you may observe some red-looking spots around the place where the dog encountered the allergen. Reddened, irritated skin and skin lesions occur due to scratching at and chewing on those itchy areas. AD is often worse during the summer, when pollen and mould levels increase.

The preferred method of handling this and any allergy is to remove the allergen from the dog. With fleas, this is comparatively easy—with pollen, it isn't. In some cases, your dog can receive a series of shots to help build up resistance, but it's not a guarantee.

Contact Allergy

In this kind of allergy, the dog reacts to an irritant that actually touches the skin. It is not as common as AD.

Flea Allergy

This is one of the most common canine allergies. Some dogs start itching madly after one flea bite. The obvious way to handle it is to make sure your dog doesn't get fleas.

Food Allergy

A food allergy is a reaction to an ingredient in your dog's food. Dogs with food allergies may scratch at their faces. Treatment involves finding the source of the allergy and removing it from the diet. In most cases, the villain is a protein, usually beef or chicken. In other cases, wheat or soy is to blame.

Hot Spots

These frightening-looking skin sores are usually caused by irritation, allergies, or dirt in the skin. The dog will scratch himself and make the condition worse by infecting the sores. If hot spots appear, wash them thoroughly with shampoo, rinse, and dry them. You may want to use a drying powder you can obtain from your vet.

Insect Stings

Unless your dog has a serious allergic reaction, a bee sting can be treated with an over-the-counter antihistamine, broken open and applied to the sting site. If your dog's breathing becomes laboured, however, he may be having an allergic reaction—get him to the vet right away.

Dogs can develop allergies to mould and pollen.

Skin Disorders

Acne

Some Bulldogs seem prone to pimples, which form on the chin or abdomen. You can usually clear them up with an over-the-counter anti-acne cream for people applied twice daily. In other cases, your vet will prescribe an oral or cream topical antibiotic. This isn't a life-threatening disease, but it can be irritating to your dog. "Puppy acne" is common in many breeds, but in Bulldogs, the condition may continue into adulthood.

Interdigital Cysts

These are chronic swellings that occur between the toes. The cysts are filled with an inflammatory fluid that is forced deep into the tissues. The cause is unknown. In a few cases, you can treat them by soaking the paw in warm water and Epsom salts, then drying it and applying a medication recommended by your vet. Most of the time, however, these cysts must be removed surgically.

Itching (Pruritus)

Itching is really a symptom, not a disease in itself. However, when a dog starts scratching from whatever cause, he can inflame the skin even further. Some dogs have a higher "itch threshold" than others and almost never scratch, no matter what torments them. For others, it's the least little thing. (It's the same with people.) Itching can be especially serious with Bulldogs, because some of them have a tendency toward self-mutilation.

Bacterial or yeast infections, hot spots, skin parasites (mites and fleas), pyoderma, and allergies are major causes of itching. If your dog starts itching, check some of these probable causes. If your dog is clean and parasite-free, consult your vet and investigate the matter further.

Lick Granuloma

If your dog suffers from lick granuloma, you may notice that he is licking himself raw. While it may have begun in response to a sore foot (although this is not always the case), it may have turned into a nervous habit, like nail biting in people. There also seems to be a genetic component. Most foot gnawers have experienced a stressful situation at home, such as the addition or loss of a family member, a period of lengthy confinement, or boredom. However, it's recently been suggested that a nervous or obsessive-compulsive disorder may also be responsible. (These things are always tricky. Many conditions begin as physical problems and then become psychological or vice versa.)

This is a frustrating disease to treat, and every dog needs to be assessed individually. The first step is usually to treat the dog's foot; the second is to treat the dog's mental state. For the foot, the veterinarian may prescribe a long-acting corticosteroid to stop the itching. A biopsy is recommended to confirm the diagnosis, as other conditions may appear similar. She may add wraps for the foot, an Elizabethan collar to protect it, and topical corticosteroid creams. Some dogs may also need antibiotics or other drugs.

To help your dog's mental state, you may need to do nothing more than pay more attention to him and give him things to do. This is usually a successful approach in the early stages of the problem. However, if it has developed into an obsessive-compulsive disorder, you may have to result to psychoactive drugs. Some people even swear by acupuncture. Contact your vet for more information on these treatment options.

Skinfold Dermatitis

Skinfold dermatitis is an inflammation of the facial wrinkles or wrinkles elsewhere on the body. It is common in Bulldogs, especially around the face and in the tail pocket. In some cases, the nasal folds that form just in front of the eye can be so pronounced that they actually rub against the cornea. Dogs with this condition will have watery, red, or infected eyes. The only treatment is surgery to remove, or at least decrease, the size of the folds.

Cardiovascular Diseases

Aortic Stenosis

Bulldogs are prone to aortic stenosis, a narrowing of the pathway for blood leaving the heart. Usually this narrowing occurs beneath the aortic valve of the left ventricle, in which case it is referred to as subvalvular aortic stenosis (SAS). Bulldogs are one of the breeds most disposed to this genetic condition. In a mild case, there may merely be a heart murmur. More serious cases can lead to exercise intolerance, fainting, heart failure, and even sudden death. Undue difficulty in breathing, coughing, or fainting should prompt a visit to your veterinarian. In dogs with moderate or

Deafness

Deafness is a common problem in Bulldogs. There is a link between a predominantly white coat (especially around the head) and loss of hearing. (The same condition is seen in Dalmatians, Boxers, and Bull Terriers.) No one really knows the reason, but it appears that during the embryo stage, pigment cells migrate or interact somehow with structures in the inner ear. During the first few weeks of life, the structures of the cochlea (the principal organ of hearing in the ear) degenerate. The condition may occur in one or both ears. The condition manifests itself by four weeks of age, and testing may be safely done after five weeks of age. The test used to confirm deafness is the BAER test, which can be performed without sedation.

A deaf dog can make a perfectly satisfactory pet, and many can learn hand signals with remarkable ease.

severe stenosis, exercise should be restricted. Sometimes beta-blocking drugs are helpful, but there is no way to cure the disease.

Congestive Heart Failure

Heart failure is caused by some abnormality in heart function or structure. Dogs with heart failure have less blood pumped to the muscles. It often leads to fluid retention in the lung or body cavity, a condition called "congestive heart failure," and causes difficulty breathing. Some kinds of heart failure are due to birth defects. In other cases, the heart valves degenerate. Heartworms can cause it, as can diseases of the lining around the heart. Dogs of any age or breed can develop the disease. Signs of heart failure include coughing, shortness of breath, difficult breathing, weight loss, and fatigue.

Some dogs with congestive heart failure fail to eat well, or show signs of muscle wasting. A low-sodium diet is best, but many dogs just won't eat that kind of food (which will consist mostly of vegetables). All commercial foods contain too much sodium for dogs with heart failure. However, it probably helps to add fish oil, which is loaded with important omega-3 fatty acids, to the diet. Of course, if your pet is overweight, put him on a diet to reduce the stress on his heart.

Respiratory Disorders

Dyspnea

Dyspnea is a fancy term for difficult breathing. It is not a disease in and of itself but is a sign of another problem. Dyspnea may result from heart or lung disease, pressure on the airway, infections, fluid retention, or trauma. Bulldogs are very prone to this problem. Treatment, if any, depends on the cause of the disease, so consult your vet to find out your options.

Bordetella (Kennel Cough)

Bordetella is a dog's version of the common cold. It is an airborne virus that in itself is not usually serious (although it is serious in puppies). It occurs mostly in kennelled dogs, is highly contagious, and can occur in combination with distemper, adenovirus, and parainfluenza. Symptoms include a harsh cough, often with gagging and nasal discharge of varying colours. In depression. Lyme disease is treated with a course of antibiotics.

Disc Disease

Intervertebral discs are almost like shock absorbers between the vertebrae in the spine. The outside of each disc (the annulus fibrosis) is tough and fibrous, but inside the disc (the nucleus pulposus), it's more like a gel. As your dog ages, the discs becomes less resilient, and they are more likely to rupture. This is what's sometimes called a slipped disc, even though nothing has actually slipped. Surgery is frequently required in more serious cases. In less severe cases, the dog may recover by himself.

Renal System Disorders

The renal system consists of the kidneys and urinary bladder. Its purpose is to cleanse the blood of toxins and other undesirable substances and excrete them from the body.

Bladder Stones

One of the most common problems of the renal system is bladder stones (uroliths), which come about when the dog's urine is saturated with excess minerals like magnesium, phosphorus, calcium, or ammonia. Bladder stones can often be prevented and are sometimes eliminated through a diet change, although some kinds are formed in the presence of bacteria such as E. coli, Staph. spp., and proteus. Some diseases, such as liver shunts, or even some medications, are also associated with the manifestation of bladder stones.

One way to check if your dog is in danger of bladder stones is to measure his urine pH, which indicates acidity. A pH of 7 is neutral. Some bladder stones tend to form in more alkaline urine, and others form in more acid urine.

To help prevent your dog from getting bladder stones, make sure he is allowed to urinate when he needs to. Keeping dogs locked up in the house for many hours a day without the chance to urinate is not only very uncomfortable for your dog, but it is just asking for bladder stones. Your dog also needs access to fresh water at all times.

Dogs with bladder stones may require surgery.

No Jumping!

Don't allow your young Bulldog to jump on and off furniture, because it is very bad for his growing bones. He could develop carpal injuries or a severe sprain. The Bulldog's body cannot withstand jumping well.

Chronic Renal Disease

Chronic renal disease is a common problem in older Bulldogs. It has no specific cause but occurs when the filtration areas or glomeruli inside the kidney deteriorate and can no longer remove normal wastes from the bloodstream. Symptoms of chronic renal disease develop slowly over time and may include excessive thirst, an increase in the amount of urine voided, and house soiling. Later problems may include vomiting, loss of appetite, and mouth ulcers. There's no cure, but obtaining special diets from your veterinarian can slow down the process.

Nervous System Disorders

Canine Cognitive Dysfunction (CCD)

Canine cognitive dysfunction, also referred to as cognitive dysfunction syndrome, is the most common ailment that affects the nervous system. It is signalled by a decline in learning, memory, and perception. Dogs with this disease tend to wander aimlessly, bark for no reason, forget housetraining, and become distant from their families. It has been successfully treated with l-deprenyl, an enzyme inhibitor; the drug is also used to treat Parkinson's disease. The addition of vitamins C and E, l-carnitine, lipoic acid, and fish oils may also help. There is even a diet available that has been specifically designed to help dogs with cognitive dysfunction syndrome.

Epilepsy

This brain disorder can affect any breed, although most researchers strongly suspect a genetic link. No one, however, really knows what causes epilepsy, which is why it is known as "idiopathic epilepsy," a seizure without a known cause. For a dog to be accurately diagnosed with epilepsy, other diseases must be ruled out first. These other diseases include thyroid dysfunction, head trauma, kidney or liver disease, calcium deficiency, toxins, diabetes, hypoglycaemia, brain tumours, and allergies. Encourage your vet to test for these other possibilities, especially thyroid problems, which are easily diagnosed with a special blood screening.

Epilepsy often first appears in dogs between one and three years of age. The main symptom is a seizure, either a partial seizure or a full seizure. Most seizures are quite brief, ranging between 45 seconds and 3 minutes. With partial seizures, the dog may not even lose consciousness but will simply shake his head or even run around frantically. Occasionally, however, long seizures lasting 20 minutes or more can occur in waves. This is a life-threatening situation, as the blood supply to the brain and other vital organs can be disrupted.

Although there is no cure for epilepsy, many treatments, including medication and lifestyle changes, can help. The most common drug therapy is phenobarbital, which is inexpensive. However, it can be hard on the liver, so some veterinarians are having luck with potassium bromide, which is safer, as well as some other medications. Even more promising is diazepam (Valium), which is used for cluster seizures. One of the great things about this medication is that it can be administered at home. Recurrent seizures usually require lifetime medication, which can be administered at home.

Unfortunately, about 30 percent of epileptic dogs do not respond well to drug therapy, and in these cases, owners just learn how to handle seizures as they occur. In most cases, the seizures are more frightening to the owner than to the dog. However, holistic veterinarians are trying other methods of treatment that may prove beneficial. These include homeopathic remedies, diet therapy, ear acupuncture, gold bead implants, herbal treatments, and vitamin

Rabies

Rabies is a 100 percent fatal disease affecting the nerves and brain, although not a problem in the Uk, it is prevalent throughout Euope and many parts of the world.

The most common sign of rabies in dogs is a behaviour change: A friendly dog will turn wild, or a wild animal will appear tame. By the time this change shows up, however, the animal may have already been infected for months. Once the signs appear, the animal will be dead within a matter of days.

If travelling abroad you will need to get your Bulldog vaccinated against the disease.

supplementation. Vitamins A, C, E, and choline have proved particularly helpful.

Endocrine System Disorders

Diabetes

About 1 in every 200 dogs will develop diabetes. Signs include excessive thirst, excessive urination, excessive appetite, and weight loss despite good appetite. It's most common in female dogs between seven and nine years of age. The treatment is the same as for humans—insulin.

Your vet will show you how to manage this condition in your Bulldog, as each dog's requirement is different.

Pancreatitis

The pancreas is a little organ tucked up under the stomach and small intestine. It produces enzymes needed to digest food and hormones, including insulin. Because we need all of this to live, the pancreas is pretty important!

Pancreatitis occurs when the pancreas becomes inflamed (in fact, "itis" means "inflammation") and starts leaking digestive enzymes, which can start digesting the pancreas itself. Some types of pancreatitis happen overnight, while others take a long time to develop. Both can be life-threatening.

Unfortunately, we don't usually know what causes pancreatitis, although certain risk factors have been identified. These include high fat content in the blood, obesity, infection, contaminated food, certain other diseases like diabetes or Cushing's disease, and the use of some prescription drugs. A

Seizures

If your dog is having a seizure, don't panic! It will probably last only a few minutes, although your dog may not seem "right" for some time following. If the seizure goes on for ten minutes, however, transport your dog to your vet, as irreversible brain damage can occur.

Remember the following points if your Bulldog suffers from a seizure:

• Don't place anything in your dog's mouth during a seizure. He won't swallow his tongue, but you can get badly bitten if you start fooling around with his mouth.

• Note down the time of the seizure, how long it lasts, and all relevant circumstances.

• Take all information regarding the seizure with you to the vet. It may help her determine the cause.

high-fat meal just before the onset of the disease is also common. A dog with pancreatitis may vomit, avoid food, have a change in body temperature (up or down), and experience pain in the abdomen. He may also stand in a "hunched" position. Diarrhoea and depression are common as well, as is dehydration. None of these signs, however, is a sure sign of pancreatitis; the disease is notoriously hard to diagnose. Your vet will run tests that include a check on the pancreatic enzymes for more clues. She may also take x-rays.

The only treatment for pancreatitis is supportive therapy, which usually includes feeding through IVs for a few days in order to rest the digestive system. Afterward, your Bulldog will probably be placed on a low-fat diet.

Cushing's Disease (Hyperadrenocorticism)

With this condition, the adrenal gland overproduces corticosteroids. Signs include increased appetite and thirst, excessive urination, muscle wasting, and panting. The dog may have fluid accumulating in the abdomen. Cushing's can be treated either medically (through the use of several drug therapies) or with surgery.

The kidneys are marvellously efficient. Over 75 percent of their function can be decreased before they are no longer able to detoxify the body!

Digestive System Disorders

The digestive system handles processing food from its point of consumption to its excretion from the body. Unfortunately, things can go wrong anywhere along the way.

Dental Disease

The good news is that your Bully is unlikely to get cavities. The bad news is that he is liable to experience gum disease and tartar buildup. Bad things start to happen when plaque (a sticky mixture of food particles and bacteria) starts to accumulate on the surface of the teeth. You can get rid of it with daily brushing, but if you don't, minerals in the saliva combine with plaque and form tartar or calculus, a combination of calcium phosphate and carbonate and plaque. It sticks to the tooth surface and forms a scaffold for the accumulation of even more tartar.

It only takes two or three days of not brushing for tartar to begin destroying your dog's teeth. You can't get rid of tartar by brushing, because at this point it's too late. Tartar doesn't feel good either. It's

Megaoesophagus

In this condition, which can be congenital or acquired, the oesophagus is enlarged. This is a very serious condition that leads to regurgitation of food, and consequently, aspiration pneumonia. There is no cure, but it can sometimes be managed by raising the dog's feeding position.

quite irritating to the gums and causes a nasty inflammation called gingivitis.

In later stages, tartar builds up under the gum and separates the gum from the, which will eventually loosen and fall out. Even jaw fracture can result. This is periodontal disease, and unfortunately, it's irreversible, painful, and dangerous. Periodontal disease inflames and destroys the structures that support the teeth. It is also the number one source of the bacteria that cause aspiration pneumonia. The bacteria can invade the blood stream and wreak havoc on the heart valves, liver, and kidneys.

Signs of periodontal disease usually include the following, although some signs are not apparent except with an x-ray or professional exam:

- Bleeding gums
- Gum inflammation (gingivitis)
- Chattering
- Drooling
- Lack of appetite and less interest in chewing
- Loose teeth
- Pawing at face
- Bad breath (halitosis)
- Choosing softer foods

You don't want your dog to have to experience periodontal disease. It's completely preventable. How? Brush your Bulldog's teeth every day and give him toys and treats that aid in the prevention of periodontal disease, like strong Nylabones. Also, take him to the vet for a complete dental workup twice a year. This is more often than some other breeds may need, but Bulldogs are prone to tooth-crowding and are thus more likely to be victims of periodontal disease.

Gastric Dilatation Volvulus (Bloat or G.V.D.)

In this condition, the stomach fills up with fluid and gas. If the stomach twists, which is common, a life-threatening emergency will ensue that requires immediate veterinary care. Signs of bloat can include attempts to vomit, hypersalivation, restlessness, and abdominal distention. Dogs who eat very fast and who belch or are flatulent are at increased risk.

Studies have shown that dogs fed a larger volume of food per meal (based on the median number of cups fed per kilogram of body weight per meal) have a significantly increased risk of bloat. Raised bowls also increase the risk of bloat.

To decrease your Bulldog's chances of falling victim to bloat, feed him two or more meals a day, supplement with low fat table scraps, and do not moisten dog kibble that is preserved with citric acid.

Anal Sac Disease

Dogs of all breeds and of any age may encounter anal sac problems. The anal sacs (often mistakenly called "glands") are two round organs located on each side of the anus (at the 4 and 8 o'clock positions). They exude powerful, bad-smelling secretions that apparently are used to give other dogs mating and territorial information. Every time the dog defecates, some of this material is deposited. Dogs can also empty their sacs when they are scared or overexcited.

Does your Bulldog have bad breath? He may be suffering from dental disease.

Anal sacs can be the source of a variety of problems. For example, they can become infected with bacteria, a condition referred to as anal sacculitis. They can also become impacted or overfilled, which can lead to acute discomfort and infection. Finally, anal sacs can develop tumours or foreign bodies. Signs that your dog is encountering anal sac problems include:

- Scooting the rear end along the ground
- Chewing or licking the tail base
- Clamping the tail down over the anus
- Reluctance to sit
- Difficulty passing faeces
- Redness or swelling in the area; perhaps even an open, draining sore

Obese dogs have more trouble draining their anal sacs properly than other dogs, and this inability only leads to further problems. However, an impacted anal gland must be expressed (squeezed) to remove the offending material. Some people recommend routinely emptying the anal sacs as a regular part of the grooming routine.

Dogs with a history of anal sac problems may be candidates for surgical removal, which is the only way to permanently solve the problem. Because your dog doesn't really "need" them, this is a pretty benign procedure, although it requires general anaesthesia, which always carries some degree of risk. If possible, schedule the surgery at the same time as some other, necessary surgery.

Vomiting

Dogs vomit more easily than humans because of the way they have evolved. (They'll eat anything.) Vomiting is not a disease but a sign of any one of a number of problems. In many cases, it's a dietary indiscretion and nothing at all to worry about. Sometimes, however, it can be extremely serious. Vomiting up to once a week may be normal for some dogs. If vomiting continues for more than one day, call your vet.

Diarrhoea

Like vomiting, diarrhoea can be trivial or very serious. It is often a sign of intestinal disease. If diarrhoea continues for more than a day, call your vet.

In general, human foods that should not be given to dogs include chocolate, onions, grapes/raisins, large amounts of garlic, and macadamia nuts.

Bloody Stools

Bloody stools can signify a variety of problems. In general, black or tarry stools suggest bleeding from high up in the digestive tract, such as that produced by a stomach ulcer. Redder stools indicate a problem lower down. If the stools have red blotches or streaks, the problem is most likely in the large intestine. However, keep in mind that even food colouring or a change in diet can affect stool colour. Observe the stool carefully and take a sample to the vet. Bleeding anywhere in the body can be serious.

CANINE EMERGENCIES

What seems to be a minor health problem can become a major emergency rather quickly. Dogs, especially Bulldogs, are stoic about pain, and often by the time we notice something is wrong, it is already very wrong. If any health emergencies should occur, be sure to contact your vet immediately.

Poisons

There are so many plants, drugs, and cleaning products that are poisonous to dogs, it's impossible to list them all in a book of this size. However, for a complete listing of toxic plants and other vital information, visit the Dogs Trust website at www.dogstrust.org.uk.

The following descriptions are some of the more common poisonous substances for dogs.

Acetaminophen

While helpful to humans, dogs cannot process acetaminophen (Paracetamol), and ingestion affects the liver and red blood cells. A toxic dose is 45 mg per pound of body weight—about six 375 mg capsules for a 50-pound (23 kg) Bulldog. Signs of poisoning include depression, vomiting, blood in the urine or faeces, and brown or blue mucous membranes. Death can occur in 18 to 36 hours. If your dog has swallowed Paracetamol, induce vomiting and get him to the vet, where gastric lavage, intravenous fluids, oxygen, vitamin C, and activated charcoal will be administered.

Did You Know?

Some dogs are born with anal canals that do not close properly and drain foul-smelling fluid as the dog walks around. These dogs are definite candidates for surgery.

Chocolate

Neither chocolate nor the wrapper it comes in is good for your dog. Chocolate has a high fat content and contains caffeine and theobromine, which stimulate the nervous system and can be toxic. Signs of chocolate toxicity include restlessness, hyperactivity, muscle twitching, increased urination, and panting. Because chocolate is high in fat, it can cause gastrointestinal upset like vomiting, diarrhoea, or pancreatitis.

If your dog gets into the chocolate box, call your vet. Most dogs recover quickly. Although not all kinds of chocolate are equally poisonous, you should still make sure that your Bulldog does not have access to any of them to avoid a potential problem.

Fireworks

It should be obvious that fireworks are extremely dangerous to dogs. Not only will a curious pet attempt to sniff lit fireworks, which can cause severe facial burns, but even unlit fireworks are deadly if ingested. They contain poisons like potassium nitrate and heavy metals like mercury. If your dog ingests fireworks, he may have to be hospitalised.

Potpourri

As much as many of us enjoy brewing up some potpourri, it is dangerous to curious dogs, especially puppies. Potpourri contains toxic essential oils and detergents. Signs of potpourri poisoning may include burns on the skin or mouth, lack of appetite, drooling, vomiting, difficulty breathing, and weakness.

If your dog has been poisoned by potpourri, bathe him in lukewarm water and flush out his eyes if needed. If he ingested it, try giving him some milk or water and immediately take him to the vet.

Car Accident

If your Bulldog gets hit by a car, he could be seriously injured internally, even if you don't see any marks on him. If your dog can walk, take him to a veterinary surgery. If he cannot walk, first get him and yourself out of the way of traffic, then take him to a vet. Move an immobilised dog very carefully, preferably with the help of another person by lifting him onto a towel or blanket and moving the blanket. Moving an injured dog could make his injuries worse. Remember to protect yourself, too. An injured dog can bite out of pain and fear - yes, even your dog. If your dog shows signs of extreme pain, wrap a strip of cloth gently around his muzzle to keep him from biting.

If your dog is beeding, try to stop the bleeding before you take him to the vet, or on the way while someone else drives you. Apply pressure with a towel or bandage to the wound until the bleeding stops and the wound begins to clot. This could take a while, depending on the severity of the injury. If bleeding won't stop, keep applying pressure until you can get your dog help. When the bleeding stops or slows, bandage the wound securely until you can get to the vet. In extreme cases where you can't get veterinary help right away, tie a piece of cloth above the wound, not so tight that you cut off all circulation but tight enough to help slow bleeding. (This only works on appendages.)

Even if your dog looks perfectly fine, take him to the vet anyway, just in case. The chances of internal injury are too great to risk your animal's health.

Wounds and Bleeding

If the wound is comparatively minor (no major bleeding), first remove debris and any foreign objects stuck in the wound. If you

Poison Control

If you think your pet has been poisoned contact your vet immediately and give as much information as you can.

Ask for advice on any action you should take right away.

Get your dog to the vet as quickly as possible and take along a sample of the poison which you think might have been the cause of his illness.

Your Canine First Aid Kit

Your canine first-aid kit should include the following items:

- **Antibiotic Ointment:** For minor skin infections.
- **Benadryl (either liquid or capsule):** For insect stings and allergies. Use 1 milligram per pound of dog (up to 50 mg).
- **Cotton Balls or Cotton Batting:** For cleaning ears and applying ointment.
- **Eye Wash:** For irritated eyes.
- **Hydrogen Peroxide:** To induce vomiting. Use 1 teaspoon every 15 minutes until it works.
- **Ipecac Syrup:** To induce vomiting. Use 1 teaspoon per 20 pounds (9kg) of dog every four to six hours.
- **Kaopectate:** For diarrhoea. Use one spoonful for each 20 pounds (9 kg) of dog every four hours.
- **Pain Reliever:** If you don't have a prescription, you can probably get by safely with buffered aspirin. Most Bulldogs suffer no ill effects from it. Use one tablet every eight hours.
- **Petroleum Jelly:** To protect and lubricate his nose; also to lubricate the rectal thermometer.
- **Rectal Thermometer:** Get one made for dogs. Lubricate the thermometer with petroleum jelly and insert gently; hold for about two to three minutes. Be sure you hang onto the end, as you don't want it disappearing. Normal temperature for most dogs ranges from 100.5°F to 101°F (38°C to 38.3°C).
- **Styptic Powder:** To stop bleeding from inadvertent cuts during nail trimming.

have clippers, cut the hair away from the wound site and clean the area with a cleansing solution. If soap is all you have, use that, but don't use hydrogen peroxide because it can damage the tissue. To control bleeding, apply direct pressure with a clean bandage and raise the bleeding portion higher than the rest of the body if possible.

If there is a lot of bleeding, do your best to get it under control and immediately rush your dog to the veterinarian.

Inability to Breathe

Dogs who have stopped breathing may respond to CPR. When performing CPR (cardiopulmonary resuscitation), you are giving your dog artificial respiration and chest compressions to get his heart going at the same time. If possible, it's best to have two people working: one for the breathing and one for the heart. Of course, that's not always possible. The chances of its success aren't great, but it is better than nothing.

CPR works using the ABC method: airway, breathing, and circulation.

Ear Medication

When a dog has an inflamed or infected ear, it hurts. This makes it harder to administer the soothing medication he needs, so you'll need to be careful and patient. Before you start, have the medication ready and the cap off. Try to hold the dog's head still with one hand and give the medication with the other. If you need to hold the ear open, be very gentle. Your dog will probably flinch when the medication goes in, so be prepared.

Most ear medication comes in a container with a long tube. Don't cram the tube into the ear; just hold it to the opening of the ear canal and squeeze gently. Rub the base of the ear to distribute the medicine all the way in.

Airway and Breathing

Lay the dog on his side on a flat surface. Breathing usually stops before the heart does. Sometimes people begin CPR on a dog who is actually breathing fine on his own, so it's vital to check before you start. It is actually dangerous to perform CPR on an animal who is breathing. A rising and falling chest indicates breathing is occurring. Dogs suffering from lack of oxygen have bluish gums.

If the dog is not breathing, *check the airway*. It may be blocked by a foreign object or vomit. To clear the airway, lay the dog on his side and gently tilt the head backward (if there is no neck trauma). If the airway is blocked, draw the tongue out. If that doesn't dislodge the object, sweep for foreign objects with your fingers or use pliers. (This is not recommended for humans, but it is okay with dogs.) If that doesn't work, try the Heimlich manoeuvre.

If your Bulldog is not breathing, gently pull his tongue out just a bit. Close the mouth by holding your hands around the muzzle, and tilt his head just a little to open the airway. Then, perform mouth-to-snout resuscitation. Breathe into the dog's nose four or five times, blowing just hard enough to see the chest expand. Check to see if your Bulldog is breathing. If he is still not breathing, keep trying until help arrives. You should give about 20 breaths a minute.

Circulation

To check the pulse, place your hand on the left side of the chest and feel for a heartbeat.

To work on the circulation, put your Bulldog on his back. (Most dogs should be placed on their sides, but barrel-chested dogs, like Bulldogs, need a different technique.) Use a hard surface to make the chest compressions more effective. Kneel next to the dog and place your cupped hands on top of each other over the ribs where the point of elbow meets the chest. Compress the chest about 3 inches one and a half to two times per second (five compressions for each breath). Get the dog to a vet as soon as you can.

Heatstroke

Bulldogs are in great danger of heatstroke. Heatstroke can occur any time the temperature rises above 70°F (21°C). Dogs cannot perspire except on the pads of their feet, and that's just not very efficient. Their only other method of heat exchange is panting.

Panting allows the dog to move large volumes of warm air away from the interior body to the outside. At the same time, that air moves over a wet tongue that is well-supplied with blood vessels. This also helps cool the blood. Still, dogs aren't tropical animals, and heat and humidity win out over a wet tongue. The hotter it is, the faster your dog has to pant.

This is one reason why dogs should never be left in the car in warm weather, even for a few minutes.

Heatstroke is easy to prevent. Make sure your Bulldog always has access to cool, fresh water, especially outdoors. Don't leave him outside in the heat in a shadeless area for even a short period. Exercise him only during the cooler periods of the day. If you go outside together, you might want to fill a kiddie pool with water so that he can refresh himself under your watchful eye.

Signs of heatstroke include panting, weakness, and incoordination. The dog may even look panicky and wild. His gums may be greying or dark red rather than healthy pink. Vomiting, diarrhoea, seizures, and death may follow. If you suspect heatstroke, drench your Bulldog with cool (not cold) water. If his body temperature is over 105°F (40°C), he will require hospitalisation and intravenous fluids. At that temperature, he is unable to get sufficient oxygen to his body tissues, and brain damage can occur.

Transporting an Injured Bulldog

The best way to move your injured dog depends partly on his temperament and partly on the nature of the injury. If possible, put a muzzle on the dog before attempting to move him. Even the gentlest dog can bite when injured and frightened.

If you suspect a problem with the back or neck, put the dog on a board to reduce the possibility of further injury.

For Dogs Under 30 Pounds (13kg)

If your Bulldog is a puppy or unusually small and there is no back injury, pick him up and carry him, cradling his body. (Try to prevent kicking.) Wrap him in a blanket and hold the injured side against your body. Very young dogs can also be carried in a box or pet carrier.

For Dogs Over 30 Pounds (13 kg)

If you have help, place the dog in a blanket and have each person carry one end like a stretcher. If you have no help, you'll just have to tough it out and carry the dog to the car. You can do it.

Many dog owners are exploring the world of alternative therapies.

CONVENTIONAL MEDICATION

From time to time I guarantee that your Bulldog will need some medication. Most often, your vet will give directions for its proper administration, but here are some general guidelines.

Dispensing Medication

Make sure you throw out any old medicine. In other words, when in doubt, throw it out!

Use all of the antibiotics your vet prescribes for your dog, even if you think the dog is better and doesn't need them anymore. Also, don't save them in the hope that you can use them on another dog if that one becomes sick. Antibiotics are not necessarily interchangeable. Also, follow the directions on the label and don't mix medications without checking with your vet first. The medication should be stored in its original container. Carefully observe your Bulldog for adverse reactions to any medication.

Liquids

Use a syringe if possible (without the needle, of course). You can get one from your vet. Squirt the medication into the back of the dog's mouth. Tuck the syringe neatly down the "cheek pocket" of the dog's mouth, and hold the jaws closed with the lips firmly together. Don't cram it down his throat, because you might get the medication into his lungs by mistake. Keep his head tilted upward. After giving the oral medication, stroke the throat gently.

Pills

If the medication can be given with food, wrap it in a piece of cheese and let him swallow it. If not, open his mouth and place the pill as far down his throat as possible.

ALTERNATIVE THERAPIES

Conventional veterinary medicine is no longer your only option, and many dog owners are exploring the new world of alternative therapies. If you are interested in taking this further, your vet will be able to give you further advice.

Herbal Medications

Herbalism is of growing interest to dog owners who are looking for alternatives to Western medications. There are several approaches to the study of herbs, among them traditional Chinese medicine, Western herbalism, and Ayurvedic medicine, which originated in India and the Middle East. Although each branch of herbal medicine has a slightly different emphasis, all work by helping the body maintain its own health. This approach is in contradistinction to conventional Western medicine, which has traditionally operated by focusing on the disease process rather than on wellness, although things are changing.

Using herbs as medicine is not necessarily a do-it-yourself approach. Herbalism is a complex

What to Do if Your Dog is Lost

The best steps to take to find a lost dog are taken before he is lost. First, your dog should wear a collar and identification (ID) tag. Many show dogs don't wear collars because they can rub and damage the coat at the neck. However, if your dog is not a show dog, he should not leave the house without wearing a collar and tag. The ID tag should list, at a minimum, your dog's name, your phone number and your postcode. Your dog can also be microchipped (see Chapter 3).

If your dog does become lost, first, call all local rescue centres and give them a description of your dog. Recent photos are useful. Then, take in a flyer with his picture. Put up signs around the neighbourhood as you drive around looking for him and put an ad in the local paper.

science, like conventional medicine, and best results are obtained when you visit a qualified veterinary herbalist. Many such practitioners also have a degree in veterinary medicine.

No one should approach herbal medication as a "quick fix." Most herbs act more slowly than do the potent drugs that partly derive from them. Several days may pass before the patient sees improvement. Nor are herbs some kind of "wonder drug" that will magically eliminate all of your pet's diseases. They are simply a method of treatment. Not every one will work on every disease, and some diseases have no cures at all, herbal or otherwise. In addition, many herbs lack the purity of laboratory-tested medications, and the dosages are not so precise.

Semi-sweet and baking chocolate are much more toxic than white or milk chocolate. About 12 ounces (355 ml) of semi-sweet chocolate will cause severe problems in the nervous system of the average Bulldog, while only four 1-ounce (30 ml) squares of baking chocolate can cause serious damage.

That doesn't mean, however, that herbs are of no use. They can often alleviate pain and relieve symptoms. In some cases, they can effect a cure. In other words, they have exactly the same properties as conventional medications. Too often people use both herbs and drugs to treat their dog's symptoms and are then disappointed and surprised to find out that the disease itself remains. It is always important to remember that treating a symptom and treating the underlying condition do not necessarily call for the same herbal or drug regimen.

Dosages

Just as with conventional medications, herbal dosages vary from case to case. Luckily, however, herbs are much more forgiving in this regard than are Western-style drugs. In most cases, you can administer doses to your pet roughly in proportion to the recommended human dose. (In other words, give a 50-pound dog one half as much as you would give a 100-pound [45 kg] person.) However, since dogs have a faster metabolic rate than people, you may want to increase initial dosages to an effective level. It's generally safe to do this in 10 percent increments, up to 50 percent over the recommended starting dose. Again, this is something to work out with your animal herbalist. Most herbalists also recommend that your dog take a break from herbal medication two days a week.

Herbal Diversity

Herbs act in a variety of ways, just as conventional medications do. Some are antimicrobial and help kill bacteria and fungi in the body. Others act as astringents and promote skin and bowel health. Some are sedatives, and some are diuretics. Some promote wellness of the cardiovascular tract. Some are anti-inflammatory, and some are carminatives, helping the digestive system function at its optimum level. Some help the entire immune system. Some promote healing. No brief survey can adequately describe the varied benefits of herbal medication, but it is something worthwhile for dog owners to research.

Herbal medications come in many forms. Probably the most useful is the dried bulk form. Some of these can be added directly to your dog's food. Storage time varies from herb to herb, and a lot depends on the way the herb is preserved. Read labels carefully, and don't try to store too much.

Overdoses of herbal medications can be toxic, just as with conventional medications. Signs of overdose include vomiting, diarrhoea, and itching. Simply because something is herbal doesn't mean that it cannot, at the same time, be dangerous in large doses or for certain animals. Comfrey, for example, contains a fair amount of pyrrolizidine alkaloids, which can cause liver damage in some individuals. Red clover is rich in the anti-clotting compound coumarin, which is contraindicated in dogs with clotting disorders. Other herbs contain such potentially dangerous substances as anthraquinones,

Herbs

Here are some of the most popular herbs and their common usages:

- Red Clover (*Trifolium pratense*): Skin problems, swollen lymph nodes
- Oregon Grape (*Mahonia aquifolium*): Anti-inflammatory; antimicrobial
- Yucca (*Achillea millefolium*): Reduces inflammation
- Echinacea or Coneflower (*Echinacea spp.*): Boosts the immune system
- Sage (*Salvia officinalis*): Anti-microbial
- Ginkgo (*Ginkgo biloba*): Helps the urinary tract
- Licorice (*Glycyrrhiza glabra*): Anti-inflammatory
- Raspberry Leaf (*Rubus idaeus*): Helps conjunctivitis and is an astringent
- Nettle (*Urtica spp.*): Helps conjunctivitis and dermatitis; provides vitamins and minerals
- Dandelion (*Taraxacum officinale*): Diuretic; provides vitamins and minerals
- Slippery Elm (*Ulmus fulva*): Helps relieve gastrointestinal or urinary infections
- Cayenne (*Capsicum spp*): Helps circulation
- Skullcap (*Scutellaria spp*): Helps anxiety, relieves pain
- Aloe Vera (*Aloe spp.*): Promotes healing
- Fennel (*Foeniculum vulgare*): Helps indigestion and flatulence
- Chamomile (*Matricaria recutita*): Helps indigestion and flatulence
- Burdock (*Arctium lappa*): Helps seborrhoea

saponins, sterols, tannins, and volatile oils. Never casually dose your dog with herbs any more than you would dose him with a prescription drug. Your dog may have a condition that would make such a dosage dangerous. Consult an expert first.

Please don't collect herbs in the wild. It's easy to get varieties confused, and some native plants are becoming extremely rare because they have been heavily collected. Buy your herbal medication commercially and always on the advice of an experienced practitioner.

Homeopathy

Homeopathy has become an important part of legitimate veterinary practice. As a science, it is about 200 years old, but it has been practiced as a folk medicine for centuries. Today there are 1,350 recognised homeopathic remedies. The "discoverer" of homeopathy was Samuel Hahnemann, a German doctor who found that quinine, the medicine used at the time to cure malaria, actually caused malarial symptoms when given to a healthy person.

Homeopathy works on a simple, interesting principle: "Like cures like." To cure an illness, you give the patient a very small, diluted amount of a substance that in large

When to Get to the Vet

Astute owners know when it's time to get professional help for their Bulldogs. The following signs indicate veterinary care is needed:

- Heart or respiratory trouble (difficulty breathing, blue or white gums, near-drowning)
- Trauma (broken bone, cut exposing a bone, heavy bleeding that cannot be stopped, eye injury, fight with a wild or unvaccinated animal, bullet or arrow wound, struck by car, puncture wounds, head trauma, broken tooth, fall, facial swelling, electric shock)
- Exposure to a poison
- Heat stroke or fever of 104°F (40°C) or higher
- Gastrointestinal distress (straining to relieve himself, bloat, vomiting blood, uncontrolled vomiting, choking, swallowing of a foreign object, bloody diarrhoea, tarry faeces, protruding rectum)
- Problems with the nervous system (extreme lethargy, collapse, seizures, tilted head, staggering, continuous pain)
- Inability to bear weight on one or more feet
- Continual sneezing or coughing
- Crying when picked up or touched
- Cloudy, swollen, or red eyes

amounts would produce symptoms similar to the target disease. The body responds by re-setting its systems to heal itself. The major philosophical difference between homeopathy and conventional Western medicine (which homeopaths call allopathy) is that traditional medicine usually works by introducing a completely different or foreign substance into the body to treat an illness. Homeopaths believe that this can cause more harm than good because it forces the body to deal with two problems rather than one while giving the body nothing to stimulate it to heal. Homeopaths feel that most Western medication merely eliminates symptoms; it doesn't cure the patient. And because one disease can cause many symptoms, homeopaths also believe that Western medicine tends to overmedicate by treating the products of the disease (the symptoms) rather than the disease itself. This can make the disease worse rather than better. (The classic argument for this belief is the administration of corticosteroids for skin problems. The cure can be much worse than the original disease.)

Homeopathic remedies come in pellet or liquid form. If you are using pellets and have no further directions, the right dose for most Bulldogs is four to five pellets. Smaller Bulldogs can get by with three. Most homeopathic remedies have a sweet taste, and dogs appear to enjoy them.

"Homeopathy is a very safe method of treatment for illness. Still, nothing is completely without risk. Too many people tend to use homeopathy as a last resort, and they don't give such remedies until the dog is already very, very sick. Most of these people are inexperienced in the art of homeopathy and also may give the wrong dose. A dose that is "almost" right is very wrong in homeopathy."

Never substitute homeopathic home care for qualified veterinary practice. In particular, don't attempt homeopathic remedies for an emergency condition unless you are on the road to the vet at the same time. Finally, always check with a homeopathic vet before administering homeopathic remedies designed for human beings. The dosages and applications may differ.

More About Homeopathy

All veterinary homeopaths have received traditional veterinary training.

To find a homeopath near you, check the British Association of Homeopathic Veterinary Surgeons at www.bahvs.com.

Flower Essence Therapy

Edward Bach developed this branch of alternative medicine in England early in the 20th century. Today there are about 50,000 active practitioners of the art worldwide. Although there are 38 different combinations of flower essences in Bach's pharmacopeia (and more than 200 other blends developed since then), the best known today is Bach's special blend of five flower essences. It is produced and sold under various names such as Rescue Remedy and Five Flower Formula. This particular decoction is widely marketed for its calming effect on nervous and stressed dogs.

The theory behind flower essence therapy is called resonance, and healers caution that they work best when the essence you select matches the core emotional challenges the dog faces (if you can figure out what they are). Treating only surface symptoms is futile. Nor are they designed to be a cure for physical ailments; instead, they are intended for psychological and emotional problems that can develop into physical distress. Although flower essences are usually preserved in brandy, you can also use cider vinegar.

Flower essences are usually administered in a dose of four drops four times a day. They can be rubbed into the gums or added to some bread and fed to the dog. Flower essence therapy requires frequent application, as its effects seem transient. It is often combined with other kinds of therapy, particularly herbs and essential oils.

Homeopathy, an alternative method of healing, operates on the principle that "like cures like."

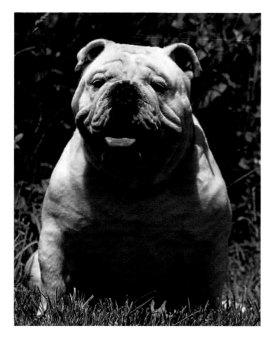

Chiropractic Therapy

Dogs who develop bone and joint problems may benefit from a visit to the veterinary chiropractor. Chiropractic treatment is not a replacement for conventional care, but it can be a valuable addition to it. Any chiropractic treatment must be agreed withh your vet. Although the benefits of chiropractic care are many, chiropractors can't work miracles. They will not be able to cure hip or elbow dysplasia, for instance. However, by carefully manipulating vertebrae, they can prevent minor spinal problems from turning into more serious ones.

Chiropractors feel for irregularities (subluxations) between vertebrae and adjust them, restoring correct vertebral alignment. Chiropractic care seems especially beneficial for disc problems and may help prevent surgery or offer valuable aftercare. Even conformation dogs, obedience dogs, and canine athletes like agility dogs can benefit from chiropractic treatment by elevating their performance to the very best level possible.

Acupuncture

Acupuncture is an age-old Chinese art that was originally designed for animals. It is ideal for dogs with arthritis, spondylosis, and hip dysplasia—in fact, most musculoskeletal disorders. It has also been used successfully in dogs with cancer, allergies, and problems in the nervous and circulatory systems.

Acupuncture involves the gentle insertion of fine needles, but dogs seldom need to be sedated for treatment. Most of them don't even notice it.

No one is really sure how or why acupuncture works. Traditional acupuncturists believe it channels the flow of Qi, a Chinese word for energy, through certain "body paths" known as meridians. Western-trained acupuncturists have a different theory. They note that the acupoints, or sites of acupuncture, usually have a thinner epidermis than surrounding tissues, and each one contains a lymph vessel, arteriole, and vein, in addition to a bundle of nerve fibres. They believe that the needles stimulate the central and automatic nervous systems, which release endorphins that lessen the perception of pain. Other acupoints may release cortisol, a natural steroid. Of course, either explanation may be true, or there may be another reason altogether.

Acupuncture has undergone further refinement with the development of electroacupuncture, a practice in which traditional needle acupuncture is combined with a microcurrent of electricity.

SENIOR DOGS

Senior dogs often have special health needs and are more prone to diseases, such as cancer and arthritis, than are younger dogs. To help keep your senior in the best of health, it's important to establish a great relationship with your vet and make sure your senior gets a checkup at least twice a year. Your Bulldog's teeth are especially in need of extra attention. Keep brushing them daily, and get them professionally cleaned as often as your veterinarian recommends.

Many older dogs have built up plenty of immunity against various diseases. Talk with your vet about stopping vaccinations or reducing their frequency.

Your senior dog will have more trouble processing food than will a younger dog. Help him out by buying top quality food, with plenty of protein. (Only seniors with poor kidney function should be on a low protein food). In fact, studies have shown that a healthy senior dog requires 50 percent more protein than a young adult! However, don't overfeed him. Obesity is a major problem in Bulldogs—especially the older fellows. Obesity will shorten his life.

If your senior has arthritis, it's important to support him with dietary supplements recommended by your veterinarian. And just because your dog is old and arthritic doesn't mean he doesn't need his exercise. He does, for both mental and physical reasons. He may not go fast, and it may take him a while to "warm up," but a walk two or three times a day will benefit his spirit, weight, and overall health.

Older dogs tend to chill easily, so keep him warm and comfortable and out of any drafty areas. Soft orthopaedic beds are particularly appreciated.

Please continue to make your older dog a part of your life. Don't exclude him now. You owe your senior Bulldog as much care now as you did when he was a playful pup. This wise old philosopher has much to teach all of us about the dignity and trials of ageing. We

Physical Therapy

Many dogs benefit from physical therapy after surgery or when plagued with a chronic condition. Most dogs can begin physical therapy within 48 hours after surgery, and sessions run twice weekly for four to six weeks.

A canine physical therapist may be a veterinarian, licenced veterinary technician, or licenced human physical therapist with special training in canine therapy. If you find a regular physical therapist who is certified to practice on animals, make sure she will work in partnership with your vet for the best outcome for your dog.

Types of physical therapy include:

- *Hydrotherapy:* Provides an almost weightless environment to improve range of motion and muscle strength, usually by means of an underwater treadmill. These are still rare, but expect their use to increase.

- *Therapeutic ultrasound:* Conducts high-frequency sound waves to muscles to reduce pain and muscle spasms. It also enhances collagen production, increases blood flow, and speeds wound healing.

- *Neuromuscular stimulation:* Uses electrical stimulation to help dogs regain muscle function and improve range of motion.

- *Passive range of motion therapies:* Involve manipulating the dog's limbs and joints in an effort to stimulate blood flow and increase range of motion in weak or paralysed limbs.

- *Therapeutic exercises:* Build muscle, recover balance, and strengthen the cardiovascular system.

would do well to listen.

Saying Goodbye

When your Bulldog does reach the stage where he no longer enjoys quality of life and has pain that can't be managed, you may have to consider whether it is time to euthanise him. This is one of the toughest decisions pet owners ever have to make. People who go through this and have a close relationship with their pet often say that they knew when their pet was ready o go. This varies immensely between pets, and their people. Some can't seem to tolerate suffering, while others seem to want to hold on for a while. Just remember to base your actions on what is best for your Bulldog, not yourself. Your veterinary surgeon can help you to make this difficult decision.

Living with an ageing Bulldog isn't always easy. Expensive treatments, low energy, behavioural changes, loss of bladder and bowel control, confusion and lack of mobility can all make the pet owner's life more difficult. But remember how much your Bulldog has given you throughout his lifetime. Our dogs love us and devote their lives to us. When they age or become ill, you have the opportunity to give back just a fraction of the love your Bulldog has given you. Getting the chance to be loved by a Bulldog is a rare and wonderful thing.

Senior dogs have special needs that should be monitored and addressed by a qualified veterinarian.

But losing a Bulldog is difficult and can involve serious prolonged grief. Give yourself time to recover. Let yourself reflect back on the good times. Seek help, in the form of the many resources for pet loss in bookstores and on the Internet. Talk to a counsellor if you feel unable to get past your grief, and know that you are not alone.

Finally, remember how very lucky you are that a Bulldog has changed your life. A dog loved you, and that means something.

RESOURCES

ORGANISATIONS

BREED CLUBS AND KENNEL CLUBS

The British Bulldog Club
www.britishbulldogclub.co.uk

The Bulldog Club Incorporated
www.bulldot-inc.com

The Kennel Club
1 Clarges Street
London W1J 8AB
Telephone: 0870 606 6750
Fax: 0207 518 1058
www.the-kennel-club.org.uk

American Kennel Club (AKC)
5580 Centerview Drive
Raleigh, NC 27606
Telephone: (919) 233-9767
Fax: (919) 233-3627
E-mail: info@akc.org
www.akc.org

Canadian Kennel Club (CKC)
89 Skyway Avenue, Suite 100
Etobicoke, Ontario M9W 6R4
Telephone: (416) 675-5511
Fax: (416) 675-6506
E-mail: information@ckc.ca
www.ckc.ca

United Kennel Club (UKC)
100 E. Kilgore Road
Kalamazoo, MI 49002-5584
Telephone: (269) 343-9020
Fax: (269) 343-7037
E-mail: pbickell@ukcdogs.com
www.ukcdogs.com

Federation Cynologique
Internationale (FCI)
Place Albert 1er, 13B - 6530
Thuin, Belgique
www.fci.be

TRAINING AND BEHAVIOUR

Association of Pet Dog Trainers
(APDT)
PO Box 17
Kempsford
GL7 4W7
Telephone: 01285 810811
www.apdt.co.uk

Association of Pet Behaviour Counsellors
PO Box 46
Worcester
WR8 9YS
Telephone: 01386 751151
Email: info@apbc.org.uk
www.apbc.org.uk

British Institute of Professional Dog Trainers
www.bipdt.net

ANIMAL WELFARE GROUPS AND RESCUE ORGANISATIONS

Royal Society for the Prevention of Cruelty to Animals (RSPCA)
Telephone: 0870 3335 999
Fax: 0870 7530 284
www.rspca.org.uk

Scotish Society for the Prevention of Cruelty to Animals (SSPCA)
Braehead Mains, 603
Queensferry Road
dinburgh
EH4 6EA
Telephone: 0131 339 0222
Email: enquiries@scottishspca.org
www.scottishspca.org

British Veterinary Association Animal Welfare Foundation (BVA AWF)
7 Mansfield Street
London
W1G 9NQ
Telephone: 01207 436 2970
email: bva-awf@bva.co.uk
www.bva-awf.org.uk

VETERINARY AND HEALTH RESOURCES

British Veterinary Association (BVA)
7 Mansfield Street
London
W1G 9NQ
Telephone: 020 7636 6541
E-mail: bvahq@bva.co.uk
www.bva.co.uk

British Veterinary Hospitals Association (BVHA)
Station Bungalow
Main Road
Stockfield
Northumberland
NE43 7HJ
Telephone: 07966 901619
Email: office@bvha.org.uk
www.BVA.org.uk

British Small Animal Veterinary Association (BSAVA)
Woodrow House
1 Telford Way
Waterwells Business Park
Quedgley
Gloucester
GL2 2AB
Telephone: 01452 726700
Email: customerservice@bsava.com
www.bsava.com

INTERNET RESOURCES

The Bulldog Information Library
(www.bulldoginformation.com)
With the ability to be viewed in six different languages, this comprehensive website provides information on health care, raising, andpurchasing Bulldogs. It also includes links to international Bulldog clubs and breeders.

Responsible Dog Breeding
www.britishdogbreeders.co.uk
A cornucopia of information and pertinent links on responsible dog breeding for British breeders.

Dog Behaviour
www.dogbehaviour.com
Canine Behaviourist Gwen Bailey's site, filled with useful advice on canine behaviour, communication and relevant links.

Petfinder
www.pet-locator.co.uk
Search shelters and rescue groups for adoptable pets.

Department of Food and Rural Affairs
www.defra.gov.uk

PUBLICATIONS

BOOKS

Gagne, Tammy
Bulldogs
Interpet Publishing, 2008

Nester, Mary Ann
Agility Dog Training
Interpet Publishing, 2007

Evans, J M
What If My Dog?
Interpet Publishing 2006

O'Neill, Amanda
What Dog?
Interpet Publishing 2006

Tennant, Colin
Mini Encyclopedia of Dog Training & Behaviour
Interpet Publishing, 2005

Barnes, Julia
Living With a Rescued Dog
Interpet Publishing, 2004

Evans, J M
Book of The Bitch
Ringpress Books, 1998

Evans, J M & White, Kay
Doglopaedia
Ringpress Books, 1998

MAGAZINES

Dog World Ltd
Somerfield House
Wotton Road
Ashford
Kent
TN23 6LW
Telephone: 01233 645669

Dogs Monthly
Ascot House
High Street, Ascot,
Berkshire SL5 7JG
United Kingdom
Telephone: 0870 730 8433
Fax: 0870 730 8431
E-mail:
admin@rtcassociates.freeserve.co.uk
www.corsini.co.uk/dogsmonthly

Dogs Today
Town Mill
Bagshot Road
Chobham
Surrey
GU24 8BZ
Telephone: 01276 858880
dogstodaymagazine.co.uk
www.dogstodaymagazine.co.uk

Kennel Gazette
Kennel Club
1 Clarges Street
London
W1J 8AB
Telephone: 0870 6066750
www.the-kennel-club.co.uk

K9 Magazine
21 High Street
Warsop
Nottinghamshire
NG20 0AA
Email: mail@9magazine.com
www.k9magazine.com

Your Dog
Roebuck House
33 Broad Street
Stamford
Lincolnshire
PE9 1RB
Telephone: 01780 766199

ABOUT THE AUTHOR

In her spare time (away from her animals), Diane Morgan is an assistant professor of philosophy and religion at Wilson College, Chambersburg, PA. She has authored numerous books on canine care and nutrition and has also written many breed books, horse books, and books on Eastern philosophy and religion. She is an avid gardener (and writes about that, too). Diane lives in Williamsport, Maryland with several dogs, two cats, some fish, and a couple of humans.

PHOTO CREDITS